Guidance Rocks!

Reproducible Guidance Games and Activities for Use in Small Group Counseling & Classroom Guidance

Grades 2-8

by Kathy Cooper, MSW & Marianne Vandawalker, M.Ed.

Cover Design - Amy Rule
Layout/graphics - Elaine Callahan
Project Supervisor - Susan Bowman
Project Editing - Susan Bowman

ISBN 1-889636-75-4

Library of Congress
2005907486

10 9 8 7 6 5 4 3 2
Printed in the United States of America

P.O. Box 115
Chapin, South Carolina 29036
(800) 209-9774 • (803) 345-1070
Fax (803) 345-0888 • Email YL@youthlightbooks.com
www.youthlightbooks.com

★★★

Dedications

I am dedicating *Guidance Rocks* to Nicole and Michael with the hope that they will receive good lessons about life and relationships at their school.

—Marianne Vanderwalker

To God, who is the most important person in my life and the author of all imagination and creativity.

To Bill, who is the best part of my life and who loves and supports me in everything I do.

To my friends, who enhance my life in so many ways and allow me to share my games and activities when we get together.

—Kathy Cooper

★★★

TABLE of CONTENTS

★★

Introduction to Guidance Rocks

Guidance time with a qualified counselor is a valuable part of the school day for any age group. During this time, students are encouraged to develop social skills, good character traits, conflict resolutions, and study skills. All of these skills help students develop a healthy self-image and also help to define the emotional I.Q. of a student. The emotional I.Q. is crucial for positive interactions with students, family members, and teachers and is also widely recognized as a very important component of educational success. Therefore, instruction, practice, and application of these guidance issues are necessary to the accomplishment of a mentally and emotionally healthy and well-educated individual.

Guidance Rocks can be used in regular classroom groups or in small skill building counseling groups.

Guidance Rocks provides unique ways to encourage and promote growth in four major areas including conflict resolution, social skills, character education, and study skills. The lessons are based on active involvement, hands-on activities, and high interest subjects. These types of lessons engage the students' interest and deal with practical problems and solutions. Activities are presented in a non-threatening environment that encourages students to openly discuss their feelings using different learning styles through role-playing and modeling opportunities.

The first chapter in *Guidance Rocks* deals with resolving conflicts. This is an important skill that helps a person to gain self-confidence and develop a better self-image in the face of a bad situation. Solving conflicts is also another important aspect of problem solving, which is emphasized in every subject area and grade level because of its importance in everyday life. Teasing remarks, disputes with friends, and general conflict requires a process of reviewing information, evaluating outcomes, and choosing an appropriate response. Students face conflicts almost every day in school and it is crucial that they learn and practice how to respond to difficult situations. In order to be successful both in the present and in the future, students must learn to be successful at problem solving in order to be a good worker, a good citizen, and a good family member.

Social skills teach good manners and culturally accepted unwritten rules of behavior and thinking. These skills lead an individual to successful relationships and toward the fulfillment of life goals. Students may often become confused about social skills because the recognized "stars" in television programs, movies, and music often serve as role models but demonstrate poor social skills often for the purpose of attracting attention or monetary gain. Because of this, emphasis needs to be placed on positive social interactions and appropriate behaviors. Working on social skills helps a person to not only become successful but also to learn to see him/herself as others see them.

Good character is also viewed as a positive attribute of an educated person. In order to develop positive attributes, children must be introduced to traits such as honesty, compassion, empathy, caring, gentleness, and good citizenship. This process involves examining the role of peer pressure and learning good decision making skills for use in difficult situations. With the availability of illegal substances and the attraction to gangs, positive character is needed to ensure a successful and peaceful society. Students often look at role models taken from the Hollywood point of view and not from the perspective of real life existence. Students need to be able to recognize and see the importance of those who aren't famous or wealthy but have qualities that money can't buy, such as honesty, perseverance, and responsibility.

Study skills shine as beacons on top of the lighthouse. Setting goals, knowing the pitfalls in reaching those goals, and establishing good work habits gives the student a path to follow with benchmarks along the way. Even when situations get difficult, well-developed and enforced study skills gives the stability that is needed to keep going and obtain success.

Guidance Rocks is filled with fun, laughter, thought provoking ideas and questions which interests young people and provides them with the necessary practice to grow and change. The games and activities show students why change is needed or teaches them how to obtain the necessary strategies for changing their behaviors.

The strategies used in the book are easy to follow and many require little preparation. They may be used for classroom guidance and for small groups and most activities can be altered slightly to use with a wide range of grades. The important thing is to know your students and to be cognizant of their needs. If there are situations in the classroom that require immediate attention, the game cards and questions may be changed to "tailor" fit the situation. The main thing is to enjoy the activities and have fun with the students with a positive outcome in mind.

Most importantly, these lessons are designed to provide assurance to the students that adults are listening and understanding the circumstances they face each school day. Enjoy *Guidance Rocks* knowing you can make a difference today.

Conflict Resolution

Conflict Resolution

Conflict resolution is a crucial skill for a safe school environment. Teasing remarks and difficult situations can lead to increased absenteeism, decreased academic performance, and increased anxiety and stress for students. When students are worried, parents, teachers, counselors, and social workers also become concerned about the physical and emotional well-being of children and consequently want to develop a plan to help children feel safe at school. This plan includes enabling and empowering students to develop strategies for becoming successful in dealing with the bullies in their lives.

Such strategies are featured in this chapter and include many games and activities that present viable alternatives for helping children become successful in dealing with tough situations in their lives.

The conflict resolution games and activities in this chapter reflect every-day situations that children encounter at school. Often, the only solutions that children know are to tell the teacher or fight. However, these activities teach that there are many other positive, practical, and easy strategies that children can learn to help them be more effective in dealing with these situations. The ideas are presented in a fun game format with a high level of repetition and practice included throughout the game. Hopefully, this format will reinforce the strategies by enabling children to practice the skills in a non-threatening environment so that they can develop the necessary confidence to employ the strategy in a real life situation. The ultimate goal is for children to be successful and consequently demonstrate this success by increased attendance and academic performance.

YES OR NO BINGO

Grade Level: 2nd - Middle School

Time: 30 minutes

Purpose: To identify appropriate and inappropriate means of conflict resolution

Materials Needed: Blank Bingo Cards (reproduced for students), Conflict Resolution Strategy List (reproduced for students), Conflict Resolution Game Cards (reproduced and cut out), small green and red pieces of paper to place over bingo spaces

Object: To be the first person to get a bingo (either horizontally, vertically, four corners, entire board, etc.)

Procedures:

1. Give each student a bingo card.

2. Ask students to write one conflict resolution strategy on each square of the bingo card. Use one of the following methods in order to complete this task so that each student's card is different.
    *   Provide students with a copy of the Conflict Resolution Strategy List featured on page 10. Twenty-four strategies are listed on this sheet in an abbreviated form to make it easier to write the strategies in the blank spaces. Ask students to randomly write the strategies on their card so that they fill up each square. Ask students to write one strategy per box.
    *   Read the Conflict Resolution Strategy List to the students. Ask students to randomly write the strategies so that each of the squares on their bingo board is filled up.
    Explain that some of the strategies are appropriate conflict resolution strategies and some are inappropriate.

3. Distribute small pieces of green and red paper to each student. Make sure that each student has enough pieces to cover their bingo board, and provide each student with a fairly even number of red and green pieces. Remember that each piece of paper should be the correct size to cover only one of the bingo boxes.

4. Explain that the green paper signifies "It's a GO!" and implies that the strategy being discussed is an appropriate strategy to use for conflict resolution. This would be a "yes" strategy. Explain that the red paper signifies a "STOP" sign by implying that the strategy being discussed is an inappropriate strategy to use in conflict resolution. This is a "no" strategy.

5. Reproduce, cut out, and place the Conflict Resolution Strategy Cards, and place these in a small basket.

6. Determine the type of bingo that will win the first game, and explain this to your students. (horizontal, vertical, diagonal, four corners, etc.) Explain that students may win bingo regardless of the color of paper pieces making up their bingo line. In other words, a horizontal bingo line may consist of red and green pieces of paper.

7. Begin the game by asking a student to come to the front of the room to choose a strategy card from the basket. Explain that each card represents either a positive or negative conflict resolution strategy. Ask the student or the class to determine if the card chosen is a "yes" or "no" strategy. A "yes" strategy indicates that the technique read out loud would be an appropriate or reasonable way to deal with conflict. A "no" strategy indicates that the technique read out loud would be an inappropriate or unacceptable way to deal with conflict.

8. As students choose cards, spend time discussing each strategy by emphasizing why each strategy is appropriate or inappropriate. The full description and discussion of each strategy is featured on the Conflict Resolution Strategy Answer Sheet on page 8. Utilize this guide for discussing the consequences of using inappropriate strategies.

9. Once it has been determined if the strategy is a yes or no behavior, ask students to place a piece of paper on the strategy listed on their card. Ask students to place a red (stop) piece of paper on the bingo card if the strategy described is inappropriate or a green (go) piece of paper on the bingo card if the strategy described is appropriate.

10. Continue playing as time allows.

FOLLOW-UP:

Ask students the following questions:
1. What is your favorite conflict resolution strategy?
2. Which strategy is the easiest to do?
3. Which strategy is the hardest to do?
4. Can you think of a situation where one of the strategies would work? Describe this situation.
5. Can you think of a situation where one of the strategies would not work? Describe this situation.
6. Which one of the strategies might you use if you saw a friend being bullied?
7. Which one of the strategies might you use if you were being bullied?
8. How many strategies do you think you would try before you told an adult?

Ask each student to write down three appropriate conflict resolution strategies that he/she will try to use when a conflict arises.

Discuss the importance of developing strategies to use before a difficult situation arises.
Tell students that it is always a good idea to have several ways of dealing with problems in case one strategy does not work.

Discuss when telling an adult is necessary.

		FREE SPACE		

CONFLICT RESOLUTION STRATEGY
(ANSWER SHEET FOR LEADER OF ACTIVITY)

1. Yell at the bully - No! Although yelling might draw attention, it may get you in an even bigger fight and cause the bully to yell at you.

2. Travel in groups of friends - Yes! Especially if you tell your friends what's going on so you can be united together against the bully.

3. Count to 10 and walk away confidently. - Yes! This will often work especially if you don't look scared while you're walking away. This way you don't get in a fight and the bully doesn't know that he/she is bothering you.

4. Start crying - No! Bullies pick on students who cry. When you cry, you give them what they want. Instead, put on a strong face, tell them to leave you alone and find some other friends to talk to.

5. Talk to someone about it - Yes! Talk to parents, teachers, counselors, and friends. Work on a strategy to deal with the bully. Practice it if you need to, and then try it out.

6. Be absent from school -No! Don't let the bully get the best of you. Make a safety plan with your teacher and counselor. Make arrangements so that you don't have to be alone with the bully if possible. Work on a plan to stand up to the bully.

7. Tell the bully to stop -Yes! Bullies don't expect people to stand up to them and will usually pick on someone who seems unlikely to be on guard. They are a little surprised when someone stands up to them.

8. Look sad or scared - No! This gives bullies what they want. Bullies pick on those who act scared and weak.

9. Ignore them - Yes or No! Bullies usually want a reaction from the people they're bullying so ignoring them might lead to more bullying. On the other hand, ignoring ridiculous comments may be exactly what you need to do in some situations. Use your own judgement.

10. Use humor - Yes! Humor can defuse a tense situation. Just make sure you don't tell a joke about the bully or make fun of him or her.

11. Threaten the bully - No! The bully might get angrier and come after you.

12. Hit them in the face - No! You get in more trouble than the bully does, and the bully deserves the trouble more than you do.

13. Tell the teacher - Yes and no! You might not want to do this any time something small happens, or you'll look as if you can't handle it. On the other hand, you might want to tell the teacher if you've continually tried a lot of things and find that nothing works. Always make sure to tell the teacher if weapons or threats are involved or if you are fearful of coming to school. Remember people can't help you unless they know what the problem is, and it usually really helps to tell someone because bullies don't usually bully around adults.

14. Call them stupid - No! This will make the bully more angry.

15. Walk away - Yes! Be sure to use this strategy especially after telling the bully to leave you alone. It's usually best not to stick around and talk, but be sure to walk to a safe place with other people around. Bullies generally don't pick on people in groups and don't like being outnumbered.

16. Tell your parents - Yes. Tell them what's happening and ask for suggestions.

17. Run away from the situation - Yes and No! If you feel you're in real danger like facing a gang of bullies, run to a safe place. If you're dealing with one person and don't feel very threatened, maybe standing up to the bully would be best. Trust your instincts.

18. Tell your parents to call the bully's parents - No! Some kids become bullies because their parents bully them. The bully's parents are more likely to believe their child, not you. They might even get defensive and blame you.

19. Talk friendly and ask them to quit - Yes! Standing up for yourself without getting angry will send a message to bullies that you do not like what they are doing.

20. Put on a strong face and stand up to the bully - Yes! Bullies need to know you're not scared.

21. Plan to get even with the bully - No! You might get in trouble and this might make the bully get angry and come after you again. Besides this makes you a bully too.

22. Laugh and act like you don't care - Yes or No! Some bullies might give up if you don't look sad. Others will bully harder to get the reaction they want.

23. Practice what you'll do with a friend - Yes! Practice makes perfect. That's why people take self defense classes. They need to practice what to do so they'll be sure to remember when they're feeling nervous.

24. Agree with the bully - Yes and No! Sometimes if a bully says something silly like your ears are too big, you might say, "You're right, they are big". In this case agreeing might be a way to let the bully know that he/she is not getting the best of you. However, if the bully says your mother is stupid, you probably wouldn't want to agree with that. In this case, you may want to use another strategy.

CONFLICT RESOLUTION STRATEGY
STRATEGY LIST

1. Yell at bully
2. Travel in groups
3. Count to 10 and walk away
4. Start crying
5. Talk to someone
6. Be absent.
7. Tell the bully to stop
8. Look sad or scared
9. Ignore them
10. Use humor
11. Threaten the bully
12. Hit them in the face
13. Tell the teacher
14. Call them stupid
15. Walk away
16. Tell your parents
17. Run away
18. Call bully's parents
19. Talk friendly
20. Strong face
21. Get even
22. Laugh
23. Practice
24. Agree

CONFLICT RESOLUTION STRATEGY GAME CARDS

Yell at bully	**Travel in groups**	**Count to 10 and walk away**
Start crying	**Talk to someone**	**Be absent**
Tell the bully to stop	**Look sad or scared**	**Ignore them**

CONFLICT RESOLUTION STRATEGY
GAME CARDS

Use humor	**Threaten the bully**	**Hit them in the face**
Tell the teacher	**Call them stupid**	**Walk away**
Tell your parents	**Run away**	**Call bully's parents**

CONFLICT RESOLUTION STRATEGY
GAME CARDS

Talk friendly	**Strong face**	**Get even**
Laugh	**Practice**	**Agree**

WHERE DO YOU STAND?

Grade Level: 2nd - Middle School

Time: 30 minutes

Purpose: To familiarize students with the attitudes about anger in our society

Materials Needed: Anger Attitude Survey questions

Object: To move to one side or another of the room to express opinions about various anger statements

Procedures:

1. Explain the purpose of this activity by sharing some of the following information.
   - Many people have different beliefs about anger. Some people believe it is acceptable to hit other people. Some people think that hitting is never acceptable.
   - The courts have laws about how people who are angry with each other can and cannot treat each other.
   - Our media show many ways to deal with anger. Some ways are effective, some are ineffective. Some ideas continue to be perpetuated by the media and are actually myths.
   - It is important for you to think about this information to determine what is true and what is not.

2. Instruct students that you will be reading several statements about anger. (Twenty-five statements are listed. You may choose as many as time allows.) Students may find that they agree with some of the statements and disagree with some of the statements. After reading each statement, point out a section of the room where students can stand if they agree with the statement and another section of the room where they can stand if they disagree with the statement. Ask students to move to different sides of the room to express their opinions.

3. Once students have expressed their opinions and are standing on different sides of the room, ask each side to support their opinions. The leader may ask probing questions about the statement based on where students are standing.

FOLLOW-UP:

After students have expressed their opinions, the leader may ask some of the following questions:
- What was the most interesting thing you discovered in this activity?
- What was the most surprising thing you discovered in this activity?
- How do you think people arrive at their particular beliefs?
- Is there any danger to adhering to any of these beliefs? If so, what are the dangers?
- If a lot of people believe that violence is acceptable, what is the impact to our society?
- Which of these beliefs do you think people at our school believe?
- What are some of the normal beliefs that you see at our school?
- What do we do about the beliefs that are negative and harmful to others?
  (Choose any particular belief and ask the following questions.)
- Does this belief help people in any way?
- Does this belief hurt people in any way?

ANGER ATTITUDE SURVEY QUESTIONS
FOR
WHERE DO YOU STAND?

1. The kind of music someone listens to influences people to fight.
2. Hanging around friends who fight makes you want to fight.
3. If someone sees a lot of hitting at home and on TV, it would probably make him or her want to fight.
4. I hate it when people fight too much on TV.
5. Our school is a safe place to be.
6. Lots of people pick on people at our school.
7. There's nothing wrong with yelling and screaming when you're angry.
8. Some people are better than other people are. These people have a right to put down others.
9. Alcohol and drugs make people more likely to stay away from fights.
10. Gangs on TV make killing look as if it's okay.
11. There's nothing wrong with watching a violent movie sometimes.
12. Cursing at a friend for stealing your boy or girl friend is okay. In fact, he/she deserves it.
13. Having a temper tantrum every once in a while is normal.
14. Walking away from a potential argument is a "chicken" thing to do.
15. Sometimes you need to tell your mom and dad what you think when you're mad, even when it means yelling and screaming.
16. Fighting is a terrible thing.
17. Parents teach you a lot about how to deal with anger.
18. Friends teach you a lot about how to deal with anger.
19. It's pretty cool on TV to see people get shot all the time.
20. I wish TV wouldn't show so much fighting.
21. Some people cannot control their anger.
22. There are some occasions when a fight is the best solution.
23. I think anger should be controlled by medication.
24. Talking about your problems is a good way to handle fights.
25. Telling someone to leave you alone is not a good way to handle bullies.

WALKIE/TALKIES

Grade Level: 3rd - Middle School

Time: 30 minutes

Purpose: To learn three appropriate responses to people who are teasing you

Materials Needed: Twenty rectangles cut out and laminated (see directions in number 1), question cards reproduced and cut out

Object:
To be the first person to move to the end of the row to award their team a point
To be the team to win the most amount of points

Procedures:

1. Cut twenty small rectangles out of construction paper. (Cut each (9 x 11) piece of paper into two or three pieces.) The purpose of creating these squares is to create game pieces that will be placed on the floor for students to stand on as they play the game. If you have access to laminating, go ahead and laminate the squares so that they can be used again.

2. Place ten rectangles in a straight line for one team to use and ten rectangles in another straight line for the other group to use.

3. Divide the class into two teams.

4. Present the following three strategies for conflict resolution.
   a. Talk it in - Talk to yourself and tell yourself the truth about the situation - Use self-talk.
   b. Talk it out - Talk to the person and tell the person what you are thinking in an assertive way
   c. Walk away or take a stand - Get away from the situation before it gets worse, or stand up for what is right in the situation if you stay.
   Explain that these strategies are great for dealing with many situations. However, note that there will be a few exceptions to using these strategies. For example, explain that students always need to immediately get an adult to help when experiencing a possible fight situation or inappropriate touching, etc.

5. Explain to students that questions are organized into three categories and are more fully explained below:
   • **Talk it in:** Present the student with a situation about teasing. Ask students to respond by saying what he/she would tell him/herself about this situation. Teach students that they should not believe the things the person has said to them but should respond to the teasing by telling them a truthful statement. This is usually referred to as self-talk. For example, If someone says "Your feet are big." You might say to yourself: "Actually my feet are a pretty average size."
   • **Talk it out:** Present a situation about teasing. Ask students to respond by telling what he/she could tell the other person in this situation. Teach the students that it's always best to try to talk it out by nicely asking the person to stop. However, occasionally the student may have to be a little firmer in telling the other person to leave the other person alone. For example:

If a student says to you: "I don't like your mama." You might respond by saying "I don't appreciate you talking about my mother since you don't even know her. Please leave me alone."

- **Walk about/ Take a Stand**: Explain the importance of moving away from negative friends and negative activities when you see or hear them going on. The reason for this is to encourage students to remove themselves from potentially dangerous situations. The secret is to learn when it's O.K. to stay and when you should not participate. Sometimes it's difficult to leave. Sometimes, you just need to take a stand in the group. For these situation cards, you will just tell if you should walk away or take a stand. You will also need to tell why you should walk away or how you would take a stand. If a student says, "Let's go beat up that boy on the playground." You might take a stand and respond by saying "No, let's just go play basketball instead" or you may want to remove yourself if you do not think the student will listen to you.

6. Choose one person from each team to begin the game. Ask each person to stand on the first square of his or her row.

7. Explain that the object of the game is to be the first person to move to the last square on their row. Students move on their rows by correctly answering questions using the conflict resolution strategies you have presented. Each question card has a different point value listed below the question, and students may move on the squares according to the point values listed on the question cards.

8. Consider the following example: If the question card has a three on it, ask the student to move ahead three squares. Once one student reaches the last square or passes the last square on the row, award their team ten points. If the second player has not had an equal amount of turns, this team is awarded another turn. If this student can also land on the last square or cross the line, you may also award this team ten points. If both teams have had an equal number of turns when one player crosses the last square, the game is then over for that round. Play continues by choosing two other students to begin the second round of play. (Both new students would begin at the starting line.)

9. Play continues as time allows.

FOLLOW-UP:

Talk with students about the importance of practicing these strategies with other students. Ask them the following questions:
- How hard would it be to "talk it in"?
- How hard would it be to "talk it out"?
- How hard would it be to "walk about" or "take a stand"?

To reinforce the ideas, you may want to use some of the following ideas:
- Draw pictures of students using these strategies to deal with teasing situations.
- Use role play to demonstrate some of these activities.
- Make up stories using the strategies.
- Make up a puppet show using the strategies.

WALKIE TALKIE QUESTION CARDS
Talk it in

TALK IT IN	TALK IT IN	TALK IT IN
You are stupid.	**You think you're so cool.**	**You are a big loser.**
4 points	6 points	3 points
TALK IT IN	TALK IT IN	TALK IT IN
You are a snob.	**You are a nerd.**	**You are fat.**
2 points	8 points	9 points
TALK IT IN	TALK IT IN	TALK IT IN
Your mama is a loser.	**You are too skinny.**	**Your clothes look like they came from Goodwill.**
10 points	4 points	3 points

WALKIE TALKIE QUESTION CARDS
Talk it in

TALK IT IN	TALK IT IN	TALK IT IN
Your hair looks like you cut it yourself.	**Who dresses you, your mama?**	**Your ears are too big.**
4 points	10 points	9 points
TALK IT IN	TALK IT IN	TALK IT IN
Your nose looks like a witch.	**Your shoes are cheap.**	**You stink.**
8 points	7 points	10 points

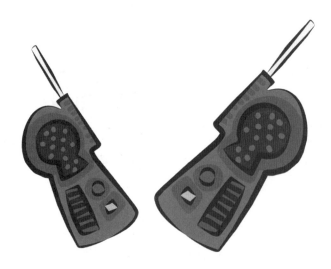

WALKIE TALKIE QUESTION CARDS
Talk it in

TALK IT IN	TALK IT IN	TALK IT IN
You are ugly. 10 points	**You are stupid.** 5 points	**You are a big loser.** 7 points
TALK IT IN	TALK IT IN	TALK IT IN
You'll be going to school here forever cause you can't pass your grade 3 points	**You throw like a girl.** (to a guy) 4 points	**You are a sissy.** (to a guy) 4 points

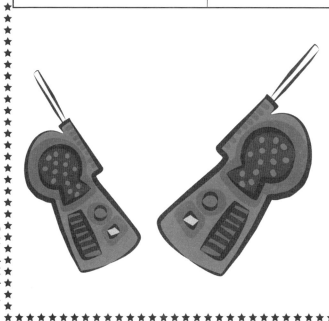

WALKIE TALKIE QUESTION CARDS
Talk it out

TALK IT OUT	TALK IT OUT	TALK IT OUT
I don't like your shirt. 1 points	**I don't think your clothes are cool.** 2 points	**I think you cheat on tests. That's why you make good grades.** 3 points
You think you're hot stuff. 4 points	**You think you're all that.** 5 points	**You are the dumbest one in the class.** 6 points
You're so goody two shoes. 7 points	**You are the teacher's pet. Who likes a teacher's pet?** 2 points	**Your mama takes drugs.** 9 points

WALKIE TALKIE QUESTION CARDS
Walk About or Take a Stand

WALK ABOUT or TAKE A STAND	WALK ABOUT or TAKE A STAND	WALK ABOUT or TAKE A STAND
Two friends are discussing plans with you for the upcoming weekend and want you to go. They want to go where older kids will be smoking pot. **5 points**	Three friends are telling funny jokes in the cafeteria about students who have problems learning. **4 points**	Three friends are telling jokes using racial slurs in the hallway. **8 points**
Four friends want to go to the movies but leave someone else out because that person is poor. **6 points**	You look across the cafeteria and think two people are staring at you. **8 points**	One girl is always staring at you in music class. **4 points**
Your friend calls somebody "gay." **10 points**	Your friend is bullying other students all the time. **9 points**	You know someone is about to beat another student up. **4 points**

WALKIE TALKIE QUESTION CARDS
Walk About or Take a Stand

WALK ABOUT or TAKE A STAND **You know someone is giving out cigarettes in class.** 7 points	WALK ABOUT or TAKE A STAND **You always see one guy giving someone else a hard time.** 3 points	WALK ABOUT or TAKE A STAND **You notice one person is being picked on in the cafeteria.** 2 points
WALK ABOUT or TAKE A STAND **You notice one person sitting by himself or herself on the playground.** 4 points	WALK ABOUT or TAKE A STAND **The conversation in your group turns to how you can get drunk.** 10 points	WALK ABOUT or TAKE A STAND **Your best friend always talks negatively about your other friends.** 4 points

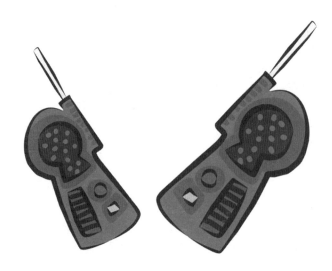

POWER POINTS

Grade Level: 3rd - Middle School

Time: 30 minutes

Purpose: To teach students various "power" strategies to use when bullies are bothering them.

Object: To be the first team to fill up the power point chart on the positive side by collecting more power points than weak points

Materials Needed: Power Point/Weak Point Chart, Power Points/Weak Points Game Cards reproduced and cut out, red squares, green squares, Situation Questions

Procedures:

1. Reproduce and cut out the power points and the weak points and place them in a basket. Make sure the cards are all mixed up the basket.

2. Cut out green and red squares from construction paper to use for the game pieces. Green squares will be given for appropriate answers or answers that are a "GO." Red squares will be given for inappropriate answers that are "STOP" responses.

3. Divide the class into small groups of 5-6 students.

4. Give each group a copy of the Power Point/Weak Point Chart.

5. Ask the students to brainstorm about certain situations when bullies can really bother them. List these on the board.

6. Ask the students to brainstorm ideas of **"Power Points"** you can use to deal with bullies. Power Points are assertive strategies that are appropriate to deal with bullies. Ask students to brainstorm **"Weak Points."** Weak Points are inappropriate responses to bullies that will not help the situation. List these ideas on the board. After students brainstorm their own Power Points and Weak Points for bullies, show the charts on pages 28 and 29 to teach students additional strategies.

7. Ask each group to choose a leader for this round. Encourage students to choose different leaders for each round. The leader's job will be to come up front to choose solutions for the problems. Ask all group leaders to come to the front of the room for each round of questions.

8. To begin the game, present a situation from those listed on page ___ . You may choose to read a situation from the list provided, or reproduce the cards and allow students to randomly choose situations. If you are having specific problems in the classroom, you may want to use these situations or some other ones that students come up with. However, regardless of what you choose, make sure that the situation involves a bullying problem or a teasing statement.

9. After reading the situation card, ask *each* group leader to randomly choose one card from the

response cards that are mixed up in the basket. Ask each group leader to read the card and decide if this is an appropriate or inappropriate way to deal with the described bullying situation. If the strategy chosen is an appropriate way to deal with a bully, ask the group leader to explain exactly how it would work when faced with that situation. Give this team member a green square if the answer is truly appropriate. (This is a "GO" solution/green card.) If the group leader draws an inappropriate response, discuss why the response might be inappropriate and give the group member a red square. (This is a "STOP" behavior/red card). Ask group members to return to their groups and put the red square on the weak point side or the green square on the power point side.

10. For additional rounds, ask a new set of group leaders to come to the front of the room, and repeat the procedure described above.

11. The winning group is the team who fills up the green square side of the power points chart first.

FOLLOW-UP:

Explain that although schools try to be safe from bullies, occasionally bullies do bother other students. It is important for all students to know how to handle these situations whether on their own or with adult intervention. The main thing students need to understand is that adults care for them and are there to protect and help them. Learning these Power Points and Weak Points will help them deal with unpleasant situations so that they can feel positive about attending school.

POWER POINTS/WEAK POINT CHART

POWER POINTS	WEAK POINTS

POWER POINTS
Appropriate Responses to Bullies

1. Stay away from bullies.
2. Travel in groups of friends.
3. Don't go to unsafe places.
4. Don't let the bullies see that they bother you.
5. Don't cry.
6. Don't act like it's any big deal.
7. Walk in the opposite direction.
8. Ask your teacher to maintain a close watch on the bully.
9. Act confident.
10. Look confident
11. Watch what's going on.
12. Tell a friend what's going on. Ask them to walk with you.
13. Tell an adult if necessary.
14. Ask an adult to help you make a plan.
15. Tell them you aren't getting in trouble by fighting.
16. Tell them you don't want to get kicked out of school.
17. Tell them you know someone will catch us, and you don't have time to get in trouble today.
18. Tell them in a tough way to leave you alone.
19. Stay calm.
20. Keep a safe distance.
21. Walk away.
22. Say "Stop it."
23. Say "Leave me alone."
24. Say "Whatever!"
25. Use humor.
26. Use I messages.
27. If you're in danger, get out of there fast.
28. Smile mysteriously and say nothing.
29. Count to 10 under your breath while just staring at them and walking off.
30. Offer a compliment.
31. Picture the rude person wearing a clown suit.
32. Walk with someone who's having problems, and help them take a stand.
33. Change the subject. Ask them if they are going to the game or saw a show on TV.
34. Agree with the bully. Tell them he/she is absolutely right.
35. Keep saying no if they want something from you.
36. Act like you can't remember the bully's name.
37. Be a broken record. Keep saying the same thing over and over.
38. Anticipate what will happen and practice what you can do.
39. Tell the bully if what they're making fun of is really a medical condition.

WEAK POINTS
Inappropriate Responses to Bullies

1. Cry.
2. Shiver.
3. Act terrified.
4. Hit!
5. Yell!
6. Kick!
7. Scream!
8. Hold your head down.
9. Call names.
10. Quit coming to school.
11. Get sick every time you see the bully.
12. Don't go in the cafeteria anymore.
13. Don't go outside any more.
14. Give the bully your lunch money.
15. Let the bully copy your paper.
16. Do whatever the bully says.
17. Run away from home.
18. Keep it all to yourself.
19. Don't get around to telling your parents.
20. Don't get around to telling your teachers.
21. Don't get around to telling your friends.
22. Continue to place yourself in dangerous situations.
23. Walk by the bully every day you can.
24. Try to change schools.
25. Start feeling depressed all the time.
26. Start letting your grades drop.
27. Start feeling scared every minute of the day.
28. Think no one can help you.
29. Play a trick on the bully.
30. Act pitiful all the time.
31. Let this problem with the bully go on for a long time.

BULLYING SITUATIONS

1. A student wants to beat you up on the playground.

2. A student asks you for your lunch money everyday.

3. A student wants you to do his/her homework.

4. A student calls you "chicken" all the time.

5. A student pulls your hair every time he/she walks by.

6. A student always accuses you of talking about him/her.

7. A student always makes fun of something about your body.

8. A student always makes fun of the way you dress.

9. A student threatens you if you don't do certain things.

10. A student doesn't want you to walk in a certain area of the school.

11. A student is always staring you down every time you walk around.

12. A student threatens to really hurt you if you tell.

BULLYING SITUATIONS
GAME CARDS

A student wants to beat you up on the playground. 	**A student asks you for your lunch money everyday.** 	**A student wants you to do his/her homework.**
A student calls you "chicken" all the time. 	**A student pulls your hair every time he/she walks by.** 	**A student always accuses you of talking about him/her.**

BULLYING SITUATIONS
GAME CARDS

A student always makes fun of something about your body.	A student always makes fun of the way you dress.	A student threatens you if you don't do certain things.
A student doesn't want you to walk in a certain area of the school.	A student is always staring you down every time you walk around.	A student threatens to really hurt you if you tell.

BUG BUSTERS

Grade Level: 2nd - 5th
Time: 30 minutes

Purpose: To teach students appropriate and inappropriate ways of dealing with conflict

Materials Needed: Lady Bug Cards, black spots cut out from construction paper, Response cards reproduced and cut out, Bug Buster Questions

Object: To be the first group to fill up their lady bugs cards

Procedures:

1. Reproduce lady bug team cards so that each group has one card. Cut out small spots from black construction paper. (Laminate the paper before cutting out the spots to make this more time efficient.)

2. Place the Bug Buster and Bug Keeper Cards in a basket. Bug Busters are those cards reflecting responses designed to make the situation better. Bug Keepers are those cards reflecting responses designed to make the situation worse.

3. Divide the class into groups of four or five. Give each group a picture of a lady bug.

4. Ask the students to tell you about things that really "bug" them. Tell them that bugs are pesky little creatures, and you have to think of good ways to get rid of them. Explain that today's lesson will deal with appropriate ways to deal with bullies who might be bugging them.

5. Review appropriate and inappropriate ways of dealing with conflict with the group.

6. After teaching the lesson, ask each group to send up one student to play the game.

7. Read a question and allow each team member to choose a response from the basket. If the answer is an appropriate way to deal with bullies, give the team member a spot to take back to place on their lady bug. If the answer is an inappropriate way to deal with bullies, do not give the student a spot. Discuss why each answer is appropriate or inappropriate.

8. Award the winning team as the team that completely fills up their lady bug card by choosing appropriate strategies and receiving spots enough to fill up their cards.

FOLLOW-UP:

A lot of things in life can bug you. The important thing to do is to develop a plan to deal with whatever it is that is bothering you. Inappropriate ways of dealing with things that bug you simply make you feel sad and like not coming to school. Use adults to help whenever most of the strategies you've learned don't seem to work.

BUG BUSTERS GAME CARDS

Telling them to stop	**Not playing with them**	**Walking away from them**
Not paying them any attention	**Ignoring them completely**	**Changing the subject**
Telling a joke	**Telling an adult**	**Looking confident**

BUG KEEPERS GAME CARDS

Crying	**Pouting**	**Staying home from school**
Feeling scare all the time	**Looking scared**	**Fighting the bully**
Giving the bully what he/she wants	**Being around the bully by yourself**	**Never telling an adult**

BUG BUSTER QUESTIONS

What do you do if someone is pulling your hair?	**What if someone calls you stupid?**	**What if someone makes fun of your clothes?**
What if someone makes fun of your new haircut?	**What if someone says you are a loser?**	**What if someone says your mama takes drugs?**
What if someone says you like somebody and you don't?	**What if someone is gossiping about you?**	**What if your friends start talking about using drugs?**

BUG BUSTER QUESTIONS

What if your friends want you to try alcohol?	What if someone said they would beat you up on the playground?	What if someone is staring at you at lunch?
What if someone wants to copy your homework?	What if someone says you are a sissy?	What if someone says you are a mama's boy?
What if someone says they won't be your friend if you don't smoke?	What if someone says if you don't fight you're a chicken?	What if someone wants you to do your homework for him or her?

LADY BUG CARDS

DON'T BE MAD, GET GLAD
Conflict Resolution Puzzle

Grade: 2nd - Middle School

Time: 15 minutes per puzzle

Purpose: To teach children lessons on conflict resolution

Materials Needed: Copies of puzzles for everyone

Object: To complete the puzzle and discover the answer

Procedures:

1. Hand out the puzzles to the class.

2. Ask the students to complete the puzzles and discover the secret messages hidden within the puzzles.

3. Share with the class the answers and discuss what the puzzle actually means.

FOLLOW-UP:

1. What were the strategies you learned to deal with conflict?
2. When will these work?
3. When will these not work as well?
4. Who are some other people you could talk to if you were worried about a bully?
5. What are some other strategies you could use with a bully?

© YouthLight, Inc.

39

DON'T BE MAD, GET GLAD

Read the question, and locate the letter corresponding to the numbers written below the blanks. You may find the letters by looking for the first number in the vertical column, the second number in the horizontal column, and the corresponding letter where the numbers intersect. Write the letters in each blank to find alternative ways of dealing with anger.

1	F	H	D	I	X
2	B	S	C	S	M
3	A	L	T	G	R
4	D	E	K	O	T
5	F	N	W	Y	U
	6	7	8	9	10

1. Whenever someone keeps teasing you and you have asked them to leave you alone, the best thing to do to prevent you from getting in further trouble is to:

   ___ ___ ___ ___   ___ ___ ___ ___
   5,8 3,6 3,7 4,8   3,6 5 8 3,6 5,9

2. Whenver you are getting angry and you feel like you might get into trouble, it's usually better to talk about the problem, your feelings, and make a plan to feel better. To do this you would have to:

   ___ ___ ___ ___ ___ ___ ___ ___ ___ ___ ___ ___ ___
   3,8 3,6 3,7 4,8 4,10 4,9 2,7 4,9 2,10 4,7 4,9 2,10 4,7

3. There are a lot of people you can talk to about your problems.
   Fill in the graph numbers of the following people who could help you with any problems you might have.

   M O T H E R   F R I E N D
   ___ ___ ___ ___ ___ ___   ___ ___ ___ ___ ___ ___

   F A T H E R   T E A C H E R
   ___ ___ ___ ___ ___ ___   ___ ___ ___ ___ ___ ___

DON'T BE MAD, GET GLAD

Answer Key

1. Whenever someone keeps teasing you and you have asked them to leave you alone, the best thing to do to prevent you from getting in further trouble is to:

W	A	L	K		A	W	A	Y
5,8	3,6	3,7	4,8		3,6	5,8	3,6	5,9

2. Whenver you are getting angry and you feel like you might get into trouble, it's usually better to talk about the problem, your feelings, and make a plan to feel better. To do this you would have to:

T	A	L	K		T	O		S	O	M	E	O	N	E
3,8	3,6	3,7	4,8		4,10	4,9		2,7	4,9	2,10	4,7	4,9	2,10	4,7

3. There are a lot of people you can talk to about your problems.
Fill in the graph numbers of the following people who could help you with any problems you might have.

M	O	T	H	E	R		F	R	I	E	N	D
2,10	4,9	3,8	1,7	4,7	3,10		1,6	3,10	1,9	4,7	5,7	1,8

F	A	T	H	E	R		T	E	A	C	H	E	R
1,6	3,6	3,8	1,7	1,7	3,10		3,8	4,7	3,6	2,8	1,7	4,7	3,10

SECRET CODE
Conflict Resolution Puzzle

Grade Level: 2nd - Middle School

Time: 15 minutes per puzzle

Purpose: To teach children lessons on conflict resolution

Materials Needed: Copies of puzzles for everyone

Object: To complete the puzzle and discover the answer

Procedures:

1. Hand out the puzzles to the class.

2. Ask the students to complete the puzzles and discover the secret messages hidden within the puzzles.

3. Share with the class the answers and discuss what the puzzle actually means.

FOLLOW UP:

1. What do you think this quote means?
2. Does trying to make friends with your enemy make sense to you?
3. Would this really work?
4. How would you do it?
5. Could you accomplish this quickly, or do you think it would take time?
6. Do you think this would always work? Why or why not?
7. What could make this not work?
8. How hard should you try before you give up?

Challenge the students to think of someone that you would like to start being friends with and how you could do this.

SECRET CODE

Two lines of letters are shown in each of the two charts. The first line in each chart represents the "uncoded" letter or the correct letter for the blank lines drawn below. The second line of each chart represents the "coded" letter written below each of the blanks below. Look at each letter written under the blanks, find it on the second line of one of the charts, and write the letter directly above this letter (on the first line) in the blank provided below. Remember that the correct answer is the letter in the first line, which is directly above the coded letter, which is found in the second line. Break this code to discover the secret answer to the question below.

Example:
C A T   *Correct letters. Look on the first line of each box.*
X Z G   *Code letters. Look on the second line of each box.*

A	B	C	D	E	F	G	H	I	J	K	L	M
Z	Y	X	W	V	U	T	S	R	Q	P	O	N

N	O	P	Q	R	S	T	U	V	W	X	Y	Z
M	L	K	J	I	H	G	F	E	D	C	B	A

Secret Question: *How do you get rid of your enemies?*

_____ _____ _____ _____ _____ _____ _____ _____ _____ _____
G   S   V   Y   V   H   G   D   Z   B

_____ _____ _____ _____ _____ _____ _____ _____ _____
G   L   T   V   G   I   R   W   L   U

_____ _____ _____ _____ _____ _____ _____ _____ _____ _____
B   L   F   I   V   M   V   N   R   V   H

_____ _____ _____ _____ _____ _____ _____ _____
R   H   G   L   N   Z   P   V

_____ _____ _____ _____ _____ _____ _____
G   S   V   N   B   L   F   I

_____ _____ _____ _____ _____ _____ _____.
U   I   R   V   M   W   H   Abraham Lincoln

43

SECRET CODE

Answer Key

Secret Question: *How do you get rid of your enemies?*

T	H	E		B	E	S	T		W	A	Y
G	S	V		Y	V	H	G		D	Z	B

T	O		G	E	T		R	I	D		O	F
G	L		T	V	G		I	R	W		L	U

Y	O	U	R		E	N	E	M	I	E	S
B	L	F	I		V	M	V	N	R	V	H

I	S		T	O		M	A	K	E
R	H		G	L		N	Z	P	V

T	H	E	M		Y	O	U	R
G	S	V	N		B	L	F	I

F	R	I	E	N	D	S.
U	I	R	V	M	W	H

Abraham Lincoln

Social Skills

Social Skills

Learning how to interact in a positive manner in the world involves a series of complicated signals that children must learn to interpret. For example, every day at school, children must constantly answer questions such as…

Was that look friendly, or did it mean that you thought I looked ridiculous?

Was that touch on the shoulder an invitation to fight or a gesture of friendship?

Was the question sarcastic or genuine?

All of these situations can be complex and based on a number of context clues involving body language and voice tone. How a child correctly or incorrectly interprets any given situation determines their response. Often if the interaction is judged appropriately, a positive social interaction occurs. However, if the situation is misread, an inappropriate or negative interaction may occur. These interactions may occur because children may have been taught to respond in certain ways at home or have been negatively influenced by media role models.

It is very important that children be taught appropriate social skills in interacting with the world around them. The games and activities in this chapter help students develop an awareness of their own actions as well as the actions of others and the resulting consequences of all of their actions. These activities will ultimately help children develop appropriate manners, respectful attitudes, and polite responses so that they can develop new skills that will enable them to have more friends, learn more effectively, and have a more positive experience at school.

THE BLUFFING GAME

Grade Level: 3rd - Middle School

Time: 30 minutes

Purpose: To identify the difference in rational and irrational ways of thinking
To identify the difference in facts and opinions

Materials Needed: Question Cards divided into two stacks -
Round 1: Rational/Irrational Cards
Round 2: Fact/Opinion Cards

Object: To win the game by obtaining the most points

Procedures:

1. Begin the activity by teaching a mini lesson to your students. Explain the concept of rational and irrational thoughts and the difference between facts and opinion to the class by teaching the following brief lesson.

Understanding rational and irrational beliefs.
* Rational beliefs express reasonable ideas and are supported by sound thinking. These beliefs usually result in moderate emotions and controlled behavior.
* For example, the following are rational thoughts and should lead to moderate emotions.
    1. I hope I have a good day. I'll try to make good choices.
    2. Everyone doesn't really have to like me, but I hope I have a lot of friends at school.
    3. If I don't make cheerleading, I'll feel bad, but I'll get over it and do something else.
* Irrational beliefs are unreasonable because they are typically supported by false or inaccurate information. These statements usually lead to extreme anger, extreme sadness, or extreme disappointment, and these emotions usually have a negative impact on the person.
* For example, the following are irrational thoughts that would possibly lead to extreme emotions.
    4 I have to make all A's, or I'm a big nobody.
    5. If I don't make the soccer team, I'm nothing but a loser.
    6. If I don't have this girlfriend, I'll never have anybody else.

Understanding facts and opinions.
* Facts can be supported with evidence and are true statements. For example, the following statements are factual.
    1. George Washington was the first president.
    2. Football is a game that many people enjoy.
    3. Mrs. Helms is my teacher.
* Opinions represent one person's feelings and may or may not represent what you think. For example, the following statements are opinions.
    4. George Washington was the greatest president in the history of the country.
    5. Football is the best sport.
    6. Mrs. Helms is not a good teacher.

These ideas and concepts are based on Albert Ellis Theory of Rational-Emotive Therapy.

Procedures:

1. Divide the class into two teams.

2. Choose one person from one team to answer the first question and ask this person to choose a question from the irrational/rational card stack. Explain that this person must answer the question and explain that the team members are not allowed to help.

3. Ask this person's team to "make a bluff." The purpose of "making the bluff" is to determine the number of points the team will receive for answering a question correctly. It will also determine how many points the team will lose when answering the question incorrectly.
   - **How to make the bluff:** Ask team members to stand if they believe the answering person has a great chance of getting the question right. Any number of team members may stand, but the team should look at their total score in order to determine how many points they can afford to lose or how many points they need to win.
   - **How to score the bluff:** If five people stand, this means that five people are "guessing" that the answering person will get the right answer. If the person does answer correctly, the team would receive five points. However, if the person gets the question wrong, the team would lose five points.
   - **How to score the bluff with points from the previous round:** If the team had achieved five points in previous rounds and the team currently has a bluff of five students, the team would then have ten points if the person gets the answer correct and zero points if the team gets the question incorrect. (Five previous points plus five points for a correct answer equals ten points. Five previous points minus five points for an incorrect answer equal zero points.)

4. Begin by playing with the Irrational versus Rational Statements from page 50. Give students one opportunity to answer. Depending on the age of the children, ask them to either answer the statement by one of the following two methods:
   - If the children are younger and you believe they may understand the answers of true and false better, use true and false instead of rational or irrational.
   - If the children are a older and can understand the concepts of rational or irrational, use this terminology.
   - Discuss the statements.

5. If the question card has a star on it, provide the answering student a choice to turn the rational statement into an irrational statement or the irrational statement into a rational statement. If the student answers correctly, award the team five additional points.
   - For example, if the statement is "If I don't make the football team, I'm no good." The statement would be irrational or false. A rational statement would be: "If I don't make the football team, I'll be sad, but I can try again next year."

6. After a predetermined time of play, change the card stacks to the fact versus opinion stack. Again, if the card has a star on it, provide the answering student a chance to turn the fact statement into an opinion statement, or the opinion statement into a fact statement for an additional five points.
   - For example, if the statement is "All girls hate me", the statement is an opinion. Someone may change the statement to a fact by saying "Maybe some girls don't like me, but I do have some friends who are girls."

7. Continue playing until time is over. Declare one team the winner by determining which team has accumulated the most points. You may also choose a predetermined amount of points and compete until one or both teams reach a predetermined number of points.

ALTERNATE METHOD OF PLAYING
This game may be divided into two sessions, using the irrational/rational cards for one session and fact/opinion cards for the other session.

FOLLOW-UP:

Focus discussion on helping students learn rational ways of looking at situations that will help them have more moderate emotions. Often students who do not get along with others or who tend to constantly experience emotions at an extreme level tend to think irrational thoughts. Working on changing these thoughts can have a profound impact in dealing with the root of many problems seen in the school environment. Learning the difference between facts and opinions can also help children in dealing with gossip and other issues between friends which tend to cause problems that interfere with academic performance.

Ask students the following questions:
1. When you hear gossip, do you always think that it is a factual statement? How can you change your thoughts?
2. When someone calls you a name, do you think that this is a factual statement? How can you change your thoughts?
3. When someone says that he or she is never going to be happy again if you don't do something, is this really true? Why not?
4. When someone says that no one likes you, is this really true? Why not?
5. When someone says that you are not cool or popular, what could you think to yourself?
6. Why is it important to control what we think?
7. Do you think that our thoughts control how we feel and act?
8. Even when it's tough to think with all the facts, how do you keep yourself from believing the false things that other people think?

RATIONAL/IRRATIONAL STATEMENTS

Directions: Depending on the age of the students, ask students to identify the statements as rational or irrational or as true (rational) or false (irrational). If the student chooses a starred question, he/she is eligible for five extra points. To receive the five points, the student is given a chance to change an irrational statement to a rational statement or a rational statement to an irrational statement.

Answer Key

1.	**Irrational/False**	When someone calls me stupid, that means that I am stupid.
2.	**Rational/True**	Even if you talk badly about my mom, I know that my mom is great anyway.
3.	**Irrational/False**	When I don't get to go to the movies, it's the worst thing to ever happen to anybody in the whole world.
4.	**Irrational/False**	Things should always go my way.
5.	**Rational/True**	For the most part, I can control the way I feel.
6.	**Irrational/False**	Since math is hard, I'll just give up because I know I'll never get anywhere in life.
7.	**Rational/True**	I wish things were easier in school, but since my classes are hard, I guess I'll just have to study really hard.
8.	**Irrational/False**	When my friend looks at me, she's probably thinking that I look stupid.
9.	**Rational/True**	I don't have to like the teacher, but I need to do what he says anyway.
10.	**Irrational/False**	You can't trust anybody.
11.	**Rational/True**	If my friend is talking about me behind my back, it is a good idea to talk to her about it.
12.	**Irrational/False**	If my friend is talking about me behind my back, she deserves to be slapped on the face.
13.	**Irrational/False**	If I don't make the soccer team, I'll be the biggest loser in the school.
14.	**Irrational/False**	If I make the soccer team, I will be the most popular kid in the school.
15.	**Rational/True**	If I work hard and make all A's, I'll be really proud.
16.	**Irrational/False**	Wearing Tommy Hilfiger or cool clothes makes you better than other people.
17.	**Irrational/False**	It's my teachers fault if I don't get an A.
18.	**Rational/True**	If someone is calling me names, I can ask him or her to stop.
19.	**Rational/True**	If someone is calling me names, I don't have to believe it's true.
20.	**Irrational/False**	If someone is misbehaving, that makes the person a big dummy.
21.	**Rational/True**	Even if I don't like someone in my class, I need to respect them and their property.
22.	**Irrational/False**	If someone is bothering me, they deserve to be hit.
23.	**Rational/True**	If someone is bothering me, I need to figure out a plan and deal with it. Hitting would not be in the plan.
24.	**Irrational/False**	If someone is staring at me, it means they think I'm ugly.
25.	**Irrational/False**	It's O.K. to hurt myself by scratching myself if I make a mistake.
26.	**Rational/True**	If someone is staring at me, they might be thinking about me or they might be thinking of something else.
27.	**Rational/True**	If my best friend talks about me, I can ask him/her about it and try to figure out the problem.

RATIONAL/IRRATIONAL CARDS

1 When someone calls me stupid, that means that I am stupid.	**2** Even if you talk badly about my mom, I know that my mom is great anyway.	**3** When I don't get to go to the movies, it's the worst thing to ever happen to anybody in the whole world.
4 Things should always go my way.	**5** For the most part, I can control the way I feel. 	**6** Since math is hard, I'll just give up because I know I'll never get anywhere in life.
7 I wish things were easier in school, but since my classes are hard, I guess I'll just have to study really hard.	**8** When my friend looks at me, she's probably thinking that I look stupid.	**9** I don't have to like the teacher, but I need to do what he says anyway.

RATIONAL/IRRATIONAL CARDS

10	**11**	**12**
You can't trust anybody. ★	If my friend is talking about me behind my back, it is a good idea to talk to her about it.	If my friend is talking about me behind my back, she deserves to be slapped on the face.
13	**14**	**15**
If I don't make the soccer team, I'll be the biggest loser in the school.	If I make the soccer team, I will be the most popular kid in the school.	If I work hard and make all A's, I'll be really proud. ★
16	**17**	**18**
Wearing Tommy Hilfiger or cool clothes makes you better than other people.	It's my teachers fault if I don't get an A.	If someone is calling me names, I can ask him or her to stop.

RATIONAL/IRRATIONAL CARDS

19	20	21
If someone is calling me names, I don't have to believe it's true.	If someone is misbehaving, that makes the person a big dummy.	Even if I don't like someone in my class, I need to respect them and their property.

22	23	24
If someone is bothering me, they deserve to be hit.	If someone is bothering me, I need to figure out a plan and deal with it. Hitting would not be in the plan.	If someone is staring at me, it means they think I'm ugly.

25	26	27
It's O.K. to hurt myself by scratching myself if I make a mistake.	If someone is staring at me, they might be thinking about me or they might be thinking of something else.	If my best friend talks about me, I can ask him/her about it and try to figure out the problem.

FACT/OPINION QUESTIONS

Directions: Identify the following as fact or opinion statements. If a question has a star on it, you may change the opinion question into a fact question or the fact question into an opinion question for an additional five points.

Answer Key

1. Opinion Pepperoni is the best kind of pizza.
2. Opinion Football is great.
3. Fact Checkers is a game.
4. Opinion Chicago is a great city.
5. Fact Charlotte is a city in North Carolina.
6. Opinion Susan is a snotty girl.
7. Opinion Fall is the best season of the year.
8. Fact There are good students in my school.
9. Opinion I am the most stupid person in my school.
10. Opinion Everybody thinks I am fat.
11. Fact Soccer is a game.
12. Opinion Math is the hardest subject in school.
13. Opinion Susan is the smartest person in the world.
14. Fact Susan makes all A's on her report card.
15. Opinion John doesn't like me because of the way I dress.
16. Fact Hard work pays off in school.
17. Fact Good grades help you get ready for college.
18. Opinion Adidas shoes are the best.
19. Fact Nike shoes are a brand on the market.
20. Opinion Tommy Hilfiger jeans are the coolest jeans.
21. Fact You need to do your homework to have good grades.
22. Opinion Every time someone looks at me, s/he thinks my hair looks bad.
23. Fact Taking drugs is bad for your body.
24. Opinion Only cool people smoke cigarettes.
25. Opinion Rich people are the most popular.
26. Fact Cigarette smoking can be very bad for your lungs.
27. Opinion People who don't wear nice clothes are stupid.
28. Fact Texas is a state in the United States.
29. Opinion Texas is the best state in the country.
30. Fact Hitting someone will usually get you in trouble.

FACT/OPINION QUESTION CARDS

1 Pepperoni is the best kind of pizza.	**2** Football is great.	**3** Checkers is a game. ★
4 Chicago is a great city.	**5** Charlotte is a city in North Carolina.	**6** Susan is a snotty girl.
7 Fall is the best season of the year. ★	**8** There are good students in my school.	**9** I am the most stupid person in my school.

FACT/OPINION QUESTION CARDS

10 Everybody thinks I am fat.	**11** Soccer is a game. ★	**12** Math is the hardest subject in school.
13 Susan is the smartest person in the world.	**14** Susan makes all A's on her report card.	**15** John doesn't like me because of the way I dress.
16 Hard work pays off in school.	**17** Good grades help you get ready for college. ★	**18** Adidas™ shoes are the best.

FACT/OPINION QUESTION CARDS

19	20	21
Nike shoes are a brand on the market.	**Tommy Hilfiger jeans are the coolest jeans.**	**You need to do your homework to have good grades.**

22	23	24
Every time someone looks at me, s/he thinks my hair looks bad.	**Taking drugs is bad for your body.** ★	**Only cool people smoke cigarettes.**

FACT/OPINION QUESTION CARDS

25 Rich people are the most popular.	**26** Cigarette smoking can be very bad for your lungs.	**27** People who don't wear nice clothes are stupid.
28 Texas is a state in the United States.	**29** Texas is the best state in the country.	**30** Hitting someone will usually get you in trouble.

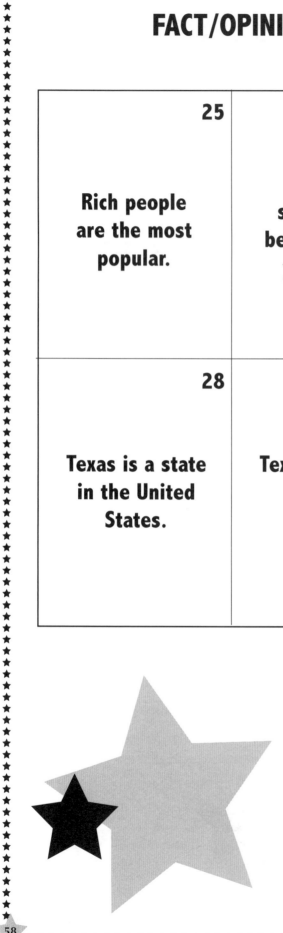

CHANGE YOUR TUNE

Grade Level: 3rd - Middle School

Time: 30 minutes

Purpose: To teach children that various responses to situations produce different actions and reactions. To teach children how important thoughts are in controlling reactions

Object: To get four straight marks in a row and win the most points by answering questions correctly

Materials Needed: Game Boards (drawn on board and explained below), dice, "What Is the Problem?" and "What Do You Do?" cards

Procedures:

1. Divide the class into two teams.

2. Draw two four by four charts on the board.

3. Ask one member from each team to come to the front. Ask each team member to randomly draw 8 plus signs and 8 minus signs on their own team's board.

Example:

Team 1

+	-	+	+
-	+	+	-
+	-	+	-
-	-	-	+

Team 2

-	-	+	+
+	-	-	+
+	+	-	-
-	+	+	-

1. Explain that the purpose of this game is to learn how actions and thoughts produce different results. The categories for the game are divided as follows:

Category 1: **What is the Problem?**
What situation has occurred that would cause a response of some kind?
(See the **What is the Problem Cards** on page 62. These cards describe six different situations that might happen to someone.)

Category 2: **What Do You Do?**
What are the different thoughts, feelings, or actions someone might exhibit in response to one of the problems listed above?
(See the **What Do You Do Cards** on page 63. These cards describe six actions describing how someone could react to the situations in the What is The Problem Cards.)

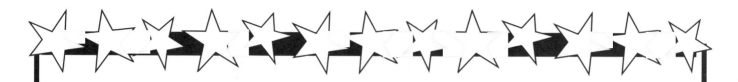

Category 3:   **What Happens?**
What happens as a result of the problem (category 1) combined with the thoughts, feelings, or actions (category 2)?
(There are no cards listed, and the students will be challenged to explain the consequences and classify these as positive or negative for purposes of this game.)

2. Ask a team member from team one to roll the die. Read the number on the die aloud, and then read the "**What is the Problem**" card that corresponds to this number. For example, if you rolled a one, read card one to the group.

3. Ask a team member from team two to roll the die. Read the number from the die aloud and then read the corresponding "**What Do You Do**" card. For example, if you rolled a six, then read card six to the group.

4. Ask both team members to explain "**What Happens**" when these two statements (What is The Problem and What Do You Do) occur simultaneously. Ask each team member to explain what might happen and whether the resulting consequence would be positive or negative.

5. For example:

    • If the first student rolls a one, the leader reads the following statement from the **"What is the Problem"** card: "The teacher says you have to stay in from playing because you've gotten in trouble."

    • If the second student rolls a three, the leader reads the following from the **"What Do You Do"** card: "You start screaming and yelling how things aren't fair and how you don't like him/her anymore."

    • Students from both teams would then be asked to discuss possible consequences of this situation and whether the consequences were negative or positive. In this situation, students might indicate that this response would likely create a "negative" consequence because it would cause the student to get in more trouble by causing the teacher to feel upset, extend the punishment, call the parents, etc.

6. Ask each team member to look at their respective game boards and cross through a minus sign if the stated consequence was negative or a plus sign if the stated consequence was positive. Explain that team members can cross out any minus or plus sign on their own board. However, the object of the game is to be the first team to cross out an entire straight line first. The straight line may include plus signs and minus signs and may run horizontally, vertically, or diagonally.

7. Ask two other team members (one from each team) to come up and repeat this process.

8. Declare the winning team to be the first team that gets a straight line of crossed out spaces either vertically, horizontally, or diagonally (like bingo). Award this team ten points.

9. Continue playing as time allows by redrawing the boards, randomly putting in the plus and minus signs, and beginning the game again.

ALTERNATE METHODS OF PLAYING:

1. Number the cards from 1-6 on the back of the card. Separate the cards into two stacks. As the students roll the die, ask them to choose and read the cards aloud to the group. Proceed as explained in the game.
2. Instead of rolling die, place the cards from category one face down. Place these cards all together on a desk or table. Place the cards from category two face down in another section of the table or desk. Ask a student from team one to choose a card from one table and a student from team two to choose a card from the other table. Proceed as explained in the game.

FOLLOW-UP:

Ask students the following questions in response to playing the game.

1. What did you notice about how the certain reactions influenced the consequences?
2. What kind of reactions produced the most positive consequences?
3. What kind of reactions produced the most negative consequences?
4. Can you control your reaction to a problem?
5. Do you have a choice about your reactions?
   • Discuss the idea that there are many choices for reactions to any event or situation and emphasize the fact that these choices always determine the consequences.
   • Encourage students to take time to think about their reactions and to consider the resulting consequences as they make decisions in their lives.
   • Continue to emphasize these concepts as you discuss literature, history, or science lessons.

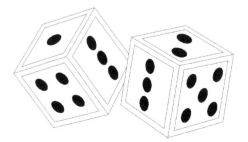

WHAT IS THE PROBLEM? CARDS

1 The teacher says you have to stay in from playing because you've gotten in trouble.	**2** Your mom asks you to clean your room, but you really want to go outside.	**3** Your grandmother says you can't go outside to play.
4 Your teacher says you have to miss music class to complete the homework assignment you forgot.	**5** You go to the store, and your dad won't let you get something that you've been wanting for a long time.	**6** Your friend says you won't be able to come over on Friday night to watch movies and spend the night.

WHAT DO YOU DO? CARDS

1 You are mad and start fussing about the whole thing.	**2** You aren't really happy, but go along with it anyway.	**3** You start screaming and yelling how things aren't fair and how you don't like him/her anymore.
4 You think to yourself, "Hey, it's not the worst thing, I'll just deal with it."	**5** You start hitting everything in sight and have a temper tantrum.	**6** You are respectful in the situation even though you're very disappointed.

LABELS

Grade Level: 3rd - Middle School

Time: 30 minutes

Purpose:
- To demonstrate the importance of getting to know people instead of pre-judging them based on previous labels.
- To promote understanding between different groups of people.

Material Needed: Descriptions copied on to address labels

Object: To treat each other as a label might imply so that students can experience what it feels like to be unfairly labeled

Procedure:

1. Divide the class into small groups of five or six.

2. Give each group a set of five or six labels. Some of the labels will be positive, and some will be negative. **Important:** Make sure that sensitive students do not get labels that ask other people to ignore them or treat them negatively. Leaders may want to code labels with a red dot for negative labels and a blue dot for positive labels, and then help to hand these out. The purpose of the activity is not to make anyone feel badly but to help them understand how others feel. Be very careful with this part of the activity.

3. Ask each person to place the label on their forehead without looking at their label.

4. Ask team members to take time to read each other's label and to become familiar with how they are instructed to treat each person. Tell group members to refrain discussing what anyone's label says.

5. Ask the group to plan a party for their class. (You can give the group any assignment to complete. For example, they can plan a school project or create a plan on how to fix a problem at the school.)

6. Ask team members to talk to each other and complete the assignment while treating each other as their labels imply.

7. Continue the activity for about ten minutes.

8. Have the students check their own label.

9. Close the activity, and ask processing questions.

FOLLOW-UP:

- How did you feel after participating in this activity?
- Was your label fair?
- If you were treated negatively by others in the group, what did you do in response?
- If you were treated positively by the group, how did your behavior change during this activity?
- Did you feel that the way you were treated had an impact on your behavior? Why or why not?
- Do you think that treating others like they are stupid makes them feel angry sometimes?
- Do you think that treating someone like they are smart makes them feel better about themselves?
- Do you think students label other students?
- Are the labels always correct?
- What could you learn about the way we treat others from this activity?
- What can you learn about the way some people act from this activity?
- What behaviors might you change as a result of this activity?

LABELS

INSTRUCTIONS: Copy the following "labels" on address labels that are small enough to be placed on a person's forehead. You may choose five or six different ones and copy all sets alike for the groups in the classroom, or you may choose to use a few different sets among the groups. If possible, try to make sure that students receive a label that is not truly representative of their personality. For example, someone who is very smart may not learn very much from receiving a "smart" label, and someone who has a learning disability may not need to get a label that implies that he/she does not know a whole lot. Be very careful!!!

I am popular. Talk to me all the time.	**I am smart. Ask me a lot of questions.**
I am angry. Act scared of me.	**I am dirty. Ignore me.**
I have a hard time learning. Treat me like I don't know very much.	**I take drugs. Treat me like I'm weird.**
I am a great athlete. Talk to me.	**I don't wear the best clothes, keep asking me where I got my clothes.**
I am rich. Act like I'm cool.	**I am poor. Act like I'm not cool.**
I don't have a lot of friends. Treat me like I'm not even here.	**I have a bad attitude. Stay away.**

GEESE CHALLENGES

Grade Level: 3rd - Middle School

Time: 30 minutes

Purpose:
- To encourage children to understand the power of working together
- To understand that some things are better accomplished when working as a team

Materials Needed: A stack of 6-8 books, 8-10 balloons, newspaper, tape, and scissors

Object: To work together to accomplish challenges

Procedures:

1. Explain that there are many things in our world that depend on everyone or everything working together to accomplish a goal. For example, geese gain a tremendous advantage from working together as can be seen in the following facts.
    a. As each goose flaps its wings, it creates an uplift for the bird that is following in the formation. By flying in a V formation, the whole flock adds 71% more flying range than if each bird flew alone.
    b. Whenever a goose falls out of formation, it suddenly feels the drag and resistance of trying to fly alone, and quickly gets back into formation to take advantage of the "lifting power" of the bird immediately in front.
    c. When the lead goose gets tired, it rotates back into the formation and another goose flies at the point position.
    d. The geese in formation honk from behind to encourage those up front to keep up their speed.

2. Ask students to brainstorm other examples of animals, places, or things that benefit from working together. For example:
    - Bees have many different jobs to make the hive work
    - Doctors, rescue workers, nurses, operating technicians, and many others work together to make a hospital work more effectively.
    - Police officers work together to keep cities safe.
    - Football teams, basketball teams, Congress, boards of directors for businesses, moms and dads, etc. all work together to accomplish a common goal.

3. Tell students that you will be doing a few experiments to discover whether working as a team really accomplishes things in better way. Ask different groups of students to complete the following challenges:

ACTIVITY 1: BOOK RELAY

Goal: To move a stack of books from one place to another with each student only carrying one book at a time.

- Ask for a group of 6-8 students to volunteer for the activity.
- Challenge the group to take a stack of 6-8 books from a designated starting point to a designated dropping off point. In this first relay, ask the first team member to take one book from the starting point to the finishing point and walk back to tag the next person in line. Ask the next person in line to take one book from the starting line to the finishing line. Continue this process until all books have been taken from the starting point to the finishing point. Time the group. Emphasize that this activity demonstrates how fast the task was done by one person at a time.
- Ask students to brainstorm a faster way to accomplish the goal. Try several ideas if you like. Try to decrease the time and emphasize teamwork.
- Try the following idea if students do not come up with it in the brainstorming session. Ask each team member to hold one book each. Ask them to stand side by side and walk together from the starting line to the finish line to place the books in a stack. Another idea might be to form a line and hand the books from the starting point to the finishing point. Time the group.

FOLLOW-UP

Ask students to answer the following questions:

a. Which procedure was faster? Why?
b. How does this challenge activity apply to the geese?
c. How can people work together to achieve a common goal?

ACTIVITY 2: BALLOON TOSS

Goal: To keep all balloons in the air for one minute.

- Choose 6-8 people to participate. Blow up the same number of balloons as you have people.
- Ask the group to stand in a circle with each student holding one balloon.
- Choose one student to stand in the center of the circle. Ask the other students to take one step backward while still holding their balloons.
- Explain that the object of this activity will be to challenge the one student in the center to keep all balloons in the air without the help of the other students in the circle. On your command, ask the other students to release their balloons in the air and time the student for one minute to see how many balloons were kept in the air for one minute. Once a balloon hits the ground, do not allow students to pick it up. Hopefully, most balloons eventually fall to the ground.
- Brainstorm a better way to keep the balloons up for one minute. Try any of the suggestions that you like. Time the group each time and count the number of balloons still in the air after one minute. Again, once a balloon falls to the ground, it is considered out of play for that round.
- Eventually, ask all students to hold their balloons. On your count, ask all students to release their balloons in the air and work together to keep all balloons in the air for one minute.

FOLLOW-UP:

1. Why was it harder to accomplish the activity during the first round?
2. Why was it easier to accomplish the activity during the second round?
3. When you have a lot on your mind, do you think it's easier to handle the problems by yourself or to allow people around you to help? (Like friends, mom, dad, grandparents, etc.)
4. What happens when people try to handle too many worries by themselves?
5. Do you think that talking to other people really helps you?
6. If someone talks to you about his or her worries, what is your responsibility? (Not to share these things with others.)

ACTIVITY 3: WRAPPING PRESENTS

Goal: To wrap a box

- Choose 3-4 people to participate in this activity. Provide newspaper, a medium size box (for wrapping), scissors, and tape.
- Ask one person to try to wrap the box while keeping one hand behind their back. This should be very difficult, so you can stop the student when it seems like it is not going to work.
- Ask the other students to put one hand behind their backs. Give them a few minutes to plan how they can wrap the package. Challenge them to complete the task in 1-3 minutes by working together.
- If the team is having difficulty, discuss ways to make it work more efficiently and allow them to try again.

FOLLOW-UP:

1. Why was it so difficult to accomplish this task with one person?
2. Why was it easier to accomplish this task with two people?
3. What made the team work together well?
4. If you have problems with a group of people, what do you do to fix the problems?

FOLLOW-UP:

* Did it seem to work better when working with groups or working alone in these activities?
* Are you ever in situations where you need to work together with a group? What skills does it take to be successful in working together as a team?
* Are you ever in situations where you need to work alone to accomplish a goal? What are some of these situations?
* What skills are necessary for you to accomplish a goal?
* What skills are necessary for you to accomplish goals with a group?
* What skills or attitudes have you seen (without mentioning names) that make it difficult for groups to accomplish their goals?

TRUE FALSE STAND UP

Grade Level: 3rd - Middle School

Time: 30 minutes

Materials Needed: Question list, one true and false card for each statement, scorekeeping pad

Purpose: To learn to pay attention to situations and make a quick assessment of the right way to respond in various situations.

Object: To receive the most amount of points by correctly answering true or false questions

Procedures:

1. Divide the class into two equal teams so that each team is sitting together on each half of the room. Ask each student to take out a piece of paper, divide it in half, & write true on one half and false on the other, and number each team beginning with one and ending with the number on each team. Therefore, team one may be numbered from 1-10 and team two numbered likewise from 1-10. Make sure there are equal numbers of students on each team and that each team member knows his/her number. If you have an unequal number of students, ask one student to choose the cards and read them to the class.

2. Ask a true or false question from the decision making question cards. After asking this question, immediately call a number from one of the teams. The numbers will represent two children - one on each team. Ask the two children, whose number you called, to immediately stand and hold the correct true or false answer to the statement. For example, if the statement is "When you are angry, the first thing you should do is pull the hair of the person who is bothering you." and you call the number "3", at this time the two children numbered "3" would immediately stand and hold up the paper with "FALSE" written on it.

3. Award the points stated on the situation card to the child's team who stands first holding the correct card.

4. Discuss why each statement may be true or false.

FOLLOW-UP:

Students have to really pay attention to hear when their number is called and must quickly come to a true or false assessment of the situation. Explain to children that this is also true in real life. They really need to pay attention to what is going on around them and quickly make good decisions. Bad decisions can get them in a lot of trouble, so they have to really be able to think fast on their feet.

DECISION MAKING QUESTION CARDS

FALSE	TRUE	FALSE
When you are in math class and someone is copying your paper, you should snatch his/her paper and throw it in the trash. 50 points	You can get an adult to help if you see someone fighting. 10 points	Being respectful to adults is a bad thing. 20 points
TRUE	TRUE	FLASE
Taking care of your property is a good thing to do. 30 points	If someone is calling your mother a name, you could try to ignore him/her, or ask him or her to stop talking about your mother. 10 points	Doing your best in school puts you on a path to drop out. 20 points
TRUE	TRUE	FALSE
Turning in all your homework is a good way to get your grades up. 30 points	Studying involves spending time doing work and reading assignments. 40 points	You are no good if you don't play football. 20 points

DECISION MAKING QUESTION CARDS

TRUE	FALSE	FALSE
Helping other people is a very good thing to do.	**If a handicapped person could not carry a lot of things, you should make fun of them.**	**If you are having problems with something, you should lie about it.**
10 points	20 points	40 points
FALSE	TRUE	TRUE
Gossiping is a great way to make friends.	**If you have good friends, you should not tell their secrets, as long as the secret isn't hurtful to them or others.**	**If someone wants you to drink alcohol from his or her parent's house, you should not try it.**
10 points	30 points	40 points
FALSE	TRUE	FALSE
If you tell someone to leave you alone in a friendly way and they don't do it, you should kick them in the knee.	**If you are in math class and someone is hitting your foot, you can ask him/her to leave you alone.**	**It's your mother's responsibility to do your homework.**
50 points	30 points	20 points

DECISION MAKING QUESTION CARDS

FALSE	TRUE	FALSE
Watching TV for 5 hours a night is a great thing to do.	Playing outside with friends is a good thing to do.	The healthiest thing to do for your body is to start smoking.
40 points	50 points	50 points
TRUE	TRUE	FALSE
Copying someone's paper will probably get you in trouble for cheating.	Being honest is a good thing.	Being kind is a bad thing.
10 points	20 points	30 points
?	TRUE	?
	Being respectful is a great thing.	
	40 points	

KARATE KIDS

Grade Level: 2nd - 5th

Time: 30 minutes

Materials: none

Purpose: To enable students to know the reasons for making appropriate decisions

Object: To demonstrate good decision making to protect yourself from disappointing consequences

Procedures:

1. Discuss the reasons for making good decisions.
   • Emphasize that one reason is to think about what others might think of you.
   • Another reason is to remember the consequences of past poor or good decisions and actions.
   • Another reason is to think how a decision will affect someone now or in the future.

2. Choose five demonstrators from the class to come to the front of the room.

3. Demonstrate the three Karate positions and share what they will represent.
   • Balancing on one foot shows the decision of waiting patiently thinking of what your parents or someone special to you would do in a difficult situation.
   • Using the 'On' move as in the Karate Kid movie (right hand moves to the right, palm faces out) shows the way to make a decision by thinking of the consequences in the future.
   • Using the 'Off' move as in the movie (left hand moves to the left, palm faces out) shows the way to make a decision by thinking of a consequence experienced in the past.

4. Read the following statement to the class.
   "I will read aloud a Karate statement. Each demonstrator needs to respond with the correct position depending on how the decision was made on the Karate Card. I will choose new demonstrators to come up front to replace each of the previous students who incorrectly demonstrate the correct answer to the Karate Card."

5. Play the game by reading the cards and evaluating the responses of the demonstrators. The demonstrators should begin with a Karate position after the Karate card is read and you have signaled the students to begin.

6. Retire any player who gets three answers correct in a row. Give each of these retiring players a round of applause.

7. Continue play as time allows.

FOLLOW-UP:

1. What helps you to think when making a decision, what others think, such as your folks at home, past happenings, or future effects?
2. Which situation was the easiest to decide the Karate position? Hardest?

KARATE STATEMENT CARDS

(Some of the statements have more than one answer.)

Matthew does his homework because he wants to make his folks proud of him. (One foot)	Sally didn't run down the hall because she remembered how she lost playtime the last time that she did that. (Left hand)	The teacher said that you might earn a bad grade if you don't study for the test. (Right hand)
Steven earned bad grades on his report card when he didn't listen to the teacher. (Left hand)	Carl can't play ball until his behavior improves in the lunchroom. (Right hand)	Sidney didn't laugh at Louise when she fell down with her lunch tray in the cafeteria because he remembered how awful he felt when he fell down the other day. (Left hand)
Mary decided not to bump into Vatasha on purpose in line since she had to go to the principal's office the last time that she had done that. (Left hand)	If you fuss or fight with someone on the school bus, you will go to see the assistant principal. (Right hand)	Alex didn't want to gossip about the new girl since Alex's folks didn't want her to treat others that way. (One foot)

KARATE STATEMENT CARDS

(Some of the statements have more than one answer.)

Tami tries to listen to the teacher since her family always wants her to have good manners. (One foot)	Maria didn't fight with Julie on the play-ground because people watching her wouldn't want to be her friend since that might scare them. (Right hand)	Dora kept a smart aleck remark to herself and ignored the class bully since the rule was that both offenders would loose playtime. (Right hand)
Toby didn't ask Jerry to give him his dessert since his folks told him that it was bad manners to ask for someone's food. (One foot)	Rhea didn't get her name on the board for bad behavior since she remembered how embarrassing it was when that happened yesterday to her. (Left hand)	Lee ran quickly to get in line when the teacher called the class in on the playground in order that he wouldn't get a bad note sent home to his folks. (Right hand)
Fortunately, Simon knew not to interrupt the teacher since his folks taught him that at home. (One foot)	Molly wanted to be able to go to a special birthday party so she kept her name off of the board by finishing all of her class work. (Right hand)	

GO FOR IT

Grade Level: 2nd - 5th

Time: 30 minutes

Materials Needed: 3 inch strips of drawing paper or adding tape, tape together if using strips of paper

Purpose: To brainstorm as many examples of good manners

Object: To draw the longest set of good manners pictures

Procedures:

1. Ask "What are some important good manners that we need?" Bring out taking turns, being neat, being polite to others, having a good attitude, watching how we eat, etc.

2. Give each student a roll or part of a roll of adding tape paper or strips of 3 inch wide plain paper that can be taped together end to end.

3. Pair the students with a good working partner. Tell them to draw pictures that show good manners and label the good manner in each picture.

4. Challenge the students to work together to try to make the longest roll of pictures of good manners.

5. Ask the students to share and compare the length of their rolls of good manner pictures two pairs at a time at the front of the room.

FOLLOW-UP:

Discuss the following questions:
Which Good Manners Skills were the easiest to draw or show?
Which ones were the most important to you?
Did it encourage you or discourage you to "Go For It" for the longest roll of pictures?

ROCKET ALERT

Grade Level: 2nd - 5th

Time: 30 minutes

Materials Needed: Construction paper, markers, 3x5 index cards, yarn, glue or hole punch

Purpose: To learn about good character traits

Object: To make a mobile

Procedures:

1. Distribute heavy weighted colored drawing paper. Ask the students to draw a rocket as large as the paper.

2. Inform the students as they work that this rocket will be turned into a mobile to hang from the ceiling to alert them to good character traits that need to be worked on everyday. The mobile will remind them of their goals.

3. Give three 3 by 5 index cards or paper that size to each student. Ask the students to stop working on their rocket and write one good character trait on each of the three cards. Ask them to draw a colorful symbol to remind them of that trait on each card. Ask each one to share his/her choices and write all of the words on the board. Give ideas of pictures or symbols that can depict that good character trait.

4. Ask the class to finish the index cards in pencil and then add color. Then encourage them to finish the rockets by cutting out the design.

5. Give each student a piece of yarn 12 inches long. Pass out the glue.

6. Demonstrate how to put the mobile together after it's colored and cut out by gluing the yarn on the end of the rocket. Then leave some space, gluing on one of the cards with glue from the top of the card to the bottom and laying the yarn in the glue. Leave more space on the yarn and glue on the next card. Lastly, leave a little more space, and then glue on the last card. Instead of glue, you may choose to use a hole punch to make holes to be able to tie the yarn into the bottom of the rocket and the top and bottom of each card.

FOLLOW-UP

Allow each student to quickly take turns holding up the rocket that he/she is working on even if it's not quite finished. Let the students read aloud the three traits on their Rocket Alert that they will try to achieve.

THUMBS UP

Grade Level: 2nd - 5th

Time: 30 minutes

Materials Needed: Thumbs Up statement sheet

Purpose: To recognize & see the importance of Good Manners

Object: To recognize Good Manners quickly

Procedures:

1. Discuss examples of Good Manners. Emphasize why these Good Manners are important in society.

2. Announce the purpose of the activity "Thumbs Up" is to discover the fastest "Thumbs Up" in the Class.

3. Invite two volunteers to come to the front of the room.

4. Explain that you will read aloud a statement that may describe good or poor manners. Ask the two volunteers to have both of their hands at their sides, and challenge each person to quickly put one thumb up in front of them if they hear a Good Manners Statement. If a thumb goes up for a poor manners statement, ask that person to sit down, and choose a new person to take his/her place.

5. Award the winner as the person who puts his/her thumb up first to a Good Manners Statement. Ask the winner to stay, and then ask the other student to choose a replacement. There may be many ties, which give extra turns for the two players at the front of the room.

FOLOW-UP:

Discuss why the Good Manners Statements are good ones to follow.

THUMBS UP STATEMENT SHEET

John likes to eat everything with his fingers. DOWN	**Jimmy does what the teacher asks him to do.** UP	**The music teacher sees everyone hold up his/her hand to answer a question.** UP
Molly throws food into other people's plates. DOWN	**Dustin brags about his good grades.** DOWN	**Mark makes fun of the team that loses.** DOWN
Sally opens up her mouth while she eats. DOWN	**Sam always says "Yes Ma'am" or "No Ma'am" to his female teacher.** UP	**Lucy throws rocks at others on the playground to get their attention. Treat others that way.** DOWN

THUMBS UP STATEMENT SHEET

Ida does her homework and turns it in on time. UP	**Phil pushes others who are in his way at the drinking fountain.** DOWN	**Dawn waits quietly in the hall.** UP
Lindsay walks quietly into the Media center. UP	**Brian helps a friend whose lunch tray fell on the floor.** UP	**Derrick spits on people.** DOWN
Harry throws paper towels on the floor in the lunchroom. DOWN	**Amber whines when the PE teacher starts a new game.** DOWN	**The class is talking while the teacher is giving directions.** DOWN

GOOD FOR YOU

Grade Level: 2nd - 5th

Time: 30 minutes

Materials Needed: skits

Purpose: To be able to recognize good & poor manners

Object: To perform in a skit on manners and select the character in the skit that has good manners

Procedures:

1. Review different examples of good manners. Discuss the importance of showing good manners to everyone. Bring out the different people in a person's life with whom you need to use good manners.

2. Tell the class that each one will be in a short situation skit about Good Manners. One of them will have good manners while the other one will show very poor or bad manners. Pair students up with a good working partner. Any extra student can help with the judging.

3. Distribute copies of the skits to each pair to practice the parts with energy and good expression. Provide three to four minutes of practice time.

4. Ask for a volunteer pair to come up to give their skit. Ask another pair to come up to stand over to the side as judges.

5. After the skit, the judges get to say "Good for you," to the one in the skit who showed good manners. The judges may wag their fingers at the person with poor manners just to add drama.

6. Continue on in this manner choosing a new pair to present their skit and a new pair of judges.

FOLLOW-UP:

Discuss after each skit the way in which the poor manners depicted in that skit would affect the whole group or other people.

SKIT SITUATION CARDS

Directions: Give each group three minutes to practice.

Two classmates are discussing the homework assignment. One has good manners & the other has poor manners.	Two friends are spending a sleep over at one of their houses. One has bad manners & the other has good manners.	Two students are in line at the water fountain. One has good manners & the other has poor manners.
One person shows another person his/her new birthday present. One has bad manners & the other has good manners.	A student brought in some cookies for snack. One student has bad manners and the other one has good manners.	There is a substitute for the day. One student has good manners & the other has bad manners.

SKIT SITUATION CARDS

Directions: Give each group three minutes to practice.

A teacher asks two students to stop running in the hall. One of the students has good manners & the other has bad manners.	**Two students are eating lunch together. One student has good manners & the other has bad manners.**	**The mother of a student comes into class. One student has good manners & the other has bad manners.**
A visitor comes into the classroom. One student has good manners & the other has bad manners.	**The class is going down the hall. One student has good manners & the other one has bad manners.**	**Everyone is in the Media Center. One student has good manners & the other one has bad manners.**

WATER SLIDE

Grade Level: 2nd - 5th

Time: 30 minutes

Materials Needed: Water Slide sheet

Purpose: To begin realizing Good Citizenship Goals

Object: To fill in the Water Slide sheet

Procedures:

1. Distribute the Water Slide sheet.

2. Challenge each student to pretend to slide into Good Citizenship by filling in the blocks on the slide describing positive traits that he/she needs to continue to work on in order to make a good splash into Good Citizenship.

3. Ask the students to share some Good Citizenship qualities as each one continues to write down the Good Citizenship quality that interests him/her.

4. Write the Good Citizenship qualities on the board as the students continue to share and write down the qualities that appeal to them.

5. After allowing enough time to fill in their slide blocks, ask the students to fill in the lines inside of the splash with ways that their lives would be better if these Good Citizenship qualities improved.

6. Discuss some ways that life would become better if they had some of the Good Citizenship qualities that are written inside of the splashes.

7. Write these examples of a better life on the board such as being happier, making parents proud, not getting into trouble, etc.

FOLLOW-UP:

Ask several students to share what they put on the Water Slide sheet and in the splash area.

SKATEBOARD

Grade Level: 2nd - 5th

Time: 30 minutes

Materials Needed: Drawing paper, pens, crayons

Purpose: To teach children good citizenship

Object: To complete a drawing

Procedures:

1. Give each student a sheet of drawing paper. Make sure the students have pencils, crayons, and/or markers.

2. Discuss ways to travel through life (for example on a skateboard), and show good citizenship. Discuss helping others, being happy, getting along with others, etc.

3. Discuss symbols or small pictures that could be drawn on a skateboard to depict or stand for these Good Citizenship qualities. For example, draw an ear for good listening, a happy face for good attitude, the peace symbol for getting along with others. Let the students share as many more as they can for a brief time.

4. Ask the students to each draw a large skateboard to cover most of the drawing paper. Put an example of a shape on the board. Tell them to draw as many symbols or pictures that show good citizenship.

5. Continue to share drawing examples as you spot them on students' papers as they draw.

FOLLOW-UP:

Permit students to stand up front in groups of three to share their skateboards and the symbols of good citizenship that seem most important to them.

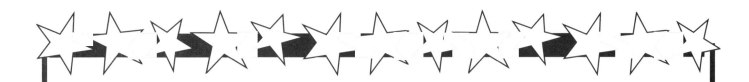

DIRT BIKE

Grade Level: 2nd - 5th

Time: 30 minutes

Materials Needed: board and markers or chalk

Purpose: To apply Good Character traits to an actual situation

Object: To fill in the most squares with the team's initials

Procedures:

1. Discuss and review different traits that make up Good Character. Discuss what good character traits you need to have in order to ride a Dirt Bike safely. Bring out responsibility, respecting others, being patient, following rules, being safe, etc.

2. Put rows of dots on the board, approximately five rows of ten dots one inch apart, as in the game of squares. Explain that students will pretend to be riding a Dirt Bike and challenge them to think up as many Good Character traits that are needed to do this safely. For example, being safe is a good character trait that a team member might say during the team's turn. That team member could then draw a line to connect two dots on the board.

3. Divide the class into two teams - certain rows versus other rows, or tables versus tables. Do this very expediently. The teams will use the first name initial of the first person on the team to put inside the squares.

4. Call on a member of each team to tell a Good Character trait that they think is important. Challenge them to think of the opposite of a Good Character trait in order to help the students to think of a good one.

5. Ask the team member who is correct to come to the board to connect any two dots on the board. These dots can later become a square as the game goes along. Then allow a member of the other team to get a chance to say a Good Character trait and to connect two dots.

6. The play continues in this manner until one of the team members closes the last two dots to make a square for the team. The team's initial goes into that square, and that team member gets an extra turn.

7. The winning team has the most squares with the team's initial in them.

FOLLOW-UP:

Have the students share which Good Character traits were the easiest and the most difficult to think up. Ask, "Are you a "square" if you try and develop these Good Character traits? Why or why not?"

RECIPE FOR DISASTER

Grade Level: 3rd - Middle School

Time: 30 minutes

Purpose: To show students the importance of following rules

Materials Needed: Ingredients for the "bad" recipe and ingredients for the "good" recipe - dependent upon the recipe you choose

Object: To show by an example what happens when you don't follow directions

Procedures:

1. Choose an easy recipe to make for the entire class that will not involve cooking. Examples might include a dip recipe for chips, an instant pudding recipe, or any other idea you might have.

2. Tell students that you will be making a fabulous recipe for the entire class to eat. Choose one student to come up front to read the recipe to you.

3. As the student reads the recipe the first time, purposely do not follow the directions called out to you. For example if the recipe calls for 1 cup of water, pour in coke or 3 cups of water. If the recipe calls for cool whip, substitute spaghetti or something else. You will come up with a ridiculous concoction that should taste terrible. As the student reads you the recipe, continue to make comments like :
    - The people who wrote that recipe don't know anything.
    - I obviously know more than they do about stuff like this.
    - I hate following recipes.
    - Recipes mess up everything.
    - Things were better before they made up all these ridiculous measurements.
    - I can do it by myself better.

4. After you finish this, ask students to come up and sample the recipe. You can play along and act like your feelings are hurt when they don't want to sample your food. Finally, ask students what the problem appears to be. Eventually lead them to the conclusion that you should have followed directions. Offer to start over and follow the directions.

5. Ask another student to read the directions for the recipe to you. This time, carefully measure and follow all directions. Ask for students to sample the product. Make sure you have enough to go around for everyone.

FOLLOW-UP:

Ask students the following questions about the activity.

1. What lesson do you think can be learned from this activity?
2. What problems occur when you don't follow instructions at school?
3. What problems occur when you don't follow instructions at home?
4. What problems occur when your parents don't follow instructions on the roads?
5. What about doctors in a hospital?
6. What about the people who purify our water?
7. What about the people who make Oreo cookies?
8. What are good reasons to follow the rules?
9. What happens in our classroom when we follow the rules? When we don't?
10. What do you think are some good things that might happen to you when you're in school and you follow the rules until you're a senior in high school? What if you don't?

Emphasize the importance of following rules in order to live in a society. Explain the importance of laws and rules to live together in a peaceful way. Discuss what happens to people who continually break the law. (prison, jail, hurt feelings, etc.) Emphasize the importance of following directions for reaching your goals.

CAREER FILL-IN

Grade Level: 3rd - Middle School

Time: 30 minutes

Purpose: To explore new careers

Materials Needed: Career puzzles, bell or something a student can ring

Object: To be the first person to push the bell. To be the first person to guess the riddle

Procedures:

1. Divide the class into two teams.

2. Invite one person from each team to come to the front of the room. Ask these students to face each other and place a bell on a small desk or table between the two.

3. Choose a game card and write the word with missing letters on the board. Keep this word covered with a piece of paper until you have read the clue about the word out loud. After you have read the clue, immediately uncover the word so that the challenge can begin.

4. After reading the clue, challenge players to consider the clues and try to think of the correct answer. Award points to the first player to ring the bell and correctly solve the puzzle within the allotted time period. If the player who first rings the bell is correct, award his/her team 10 points. If the player is incorrect, give the other team a chance to solve the word puzzle. Award this team ten points if the player can correctly guess the word. Time the players and allow only twenty seconds to solve the puzzle before play goes to the other team. (Twenty seconds for the person who rings the bell or twenty seconds to the second player trying to guess.) If neither team member can guess the word, immediately cover up the puzzle and ask the players to choose two additional teammates to come to the front. Again, repeat the process allowing these two players to compete for the points. Insist that the other team members be quiet during the challenge to make the game more exciting.

5. Award the winning team as the team that collects the most points in the allotted time period.

FOLLOW-UP:

1. What do you think is important in reaching your goals to attain your career?
2. Is education important in any of these fields?
3. Is character important in any of these fields?
4. How does your work in school affect your career choice?
5. How do your decisions now affect your career choices in the future?

FOLLOW-UP ACTIVITY:

Give the students the Career Puzzle to complete after playing the game.

CAREER FILL-IN GAME CARDS

Answer Key

1. C __ __ P __ __ T __ R (Carpenter)
   Fill in the blanks to find someone who works with wood.

2. ROTCOD __ __ __ __ __ (Doctor)
   Reverse the letters to find someone who helps people with medical problems.

3. SC__ EN__ IS___ (Scientist)
   Fill in every 3rd letter to find someone who conducts experiments.

4. P L C O F C R__ __ __ __ __ __ __ __ __ __ __ __ (Police Officer)
   Fill in every other letter to find someone who drives around and makes sure people are not speeding and helps people in car accidents.

5. C _ M__ U __ E __ P__O__R__M__E__ (Computer Programmer)
   Fill in the blanks to find someone who works in technology.

6. REKNAB __ __ __ __ __ __ (Banker)
   Reverse the letters to find someone who works with money.

7. __ __ U __ __ E __ (Plumber)
   Fill in all consonants to find someone who works with pipes and water problems in bathroom and kitchens.

8. __ __ __ __ Fighter (Fire Fighter)
   Fill in the first word to find someone who uses water to put out hot flames.

9. __ __ RM __ R (Farmer)
   Fill in letters using only letters below or preceding G in the alphabet to find someone who grows crops.

10. __ __ A __ __ECH __ICIA __ (X-Ray technician)
    Fill in letters using only letters after or following L in the alphabet to find someone who takes films in special rooms to examine broken bones.

CAREER FILL-IN GAME CARDS

1. C ____ ____ P ____ ____ T ____ R
    Fill in the blanks to find someone who works with wood.

2. ROTCOD ____ ____ ____ ____ ____ ____
    Reverse the letters to find someone who helps people with medical problems.

3. SC____ EN____ IS____
    Fill in every 3rd letter to find someone who conducts experiments.

4. P L C O F C R ____ ____ ____ ____ ____ ____ ____ ____ ____ ____ ____ ____ ____
    Fill in every other letter to find someone who drives around and makes sure people are not speeding and helps people in car accidents.

5. C ___ M ____ U ___ E ____ P ___ O ___ R ___ M ___ E ___
    Fill in the blanks to find someone who works in technology.

6. REKNAB ____ ____ ____ ____ ____ ____
    Reverse the letters to find someone who works with money.

7. ____ ____ U ____ ____ E ____
    Fill in all consonants to find someone who works with pipes and water problems in bathroom and kitchens.

8. ____ ____ ____ ____ Fighter
    Fill in the first word to find someone who uses water to put out hot flames.

9. ____ ____ RM ____ R
    Fill in letters using only letters below G in the alphabet to find someone who grows crops.

10. ____ ____ A ____ ____ECH ____ICIA ____
    Fill in letters using only letters after L in the alphabet to find someone who takes films in special rooms to examine broken bones.

CAREER PUZZLE

Grade Level: 3rd - Middle School

Time: 30 minutes

Purpose: To consider career choices

Materials Needed: one puzzle for each student or one puzzle per group

Object: To complete the puzzle

Procedures:

1. Ask students to work on puzzles individually or in groups.

2. Challenge students to complete the puzzles and then discuss the answers.

PUZZLE ANSWERS

Answer Key

1. Doctor
2. Florist
3. Nurse
4. Plumber
5. Painter
6. Teacher
7. Banker
8. Dentist

CAREER PUZZLE

Line 1   D N P F

Line 2   O U L L C R U O

Line 3   T S M R O E B I R X E S U

Line 4   P R T P T B D A E A E I A N N N

Line 5   C K T T H E I E E R S R R X T X

Make career words by recording every 4th letter following the first letter provided. Continue recording letters for the number of blanks written by the letter.

For example:

The fourth letter after the "D" in line one is the letter "O". The fourth letter after "O" is "C".

D in line 1   D ____ ____ ____ ____ ____

F in line 1   F ____ ____ ____ ____ ____ ____

N in line 1   N ____ ____ ____ ____

P in line 1   P ____ ____ ____ ____ ____

Second P in line 4   P ____ ____ ____ ____ ____

Second T in line 4   T ____ ____ ____ ____ ____ ____

First B in line 4   B ____ ____ ____ ____ ____

First D in line 4   D ____ ____ ____ ____ ____ ____

CAREER MATH PROBLEMS

Grade Level: 3rd - Middle School

Time: 30 minutes

Purpose: To consider career choices

Materials Needed: One worksheet for each student or one worksheet per group

Object: To complete the worksheet

Procedures:

1. Ask students to work on puzzles individually or in groups.

1. Challenge students to complete the puzzles and then discuss the answers.

2. Ask the students the following questions upon completion of the puzzles:

   - What are some other math careers?
   - What would happen if you didn't know very much math and you had a job that required measuring?
   - What would happen if a pharmacist did not know math?
   - What would happen if a farmer did not know math?
   - What would happen if a banker did not know math?
   - What would happen if a carpenter did not know math?
   - What skills will you need to work on to learn good math skills for the future?

CAREER MATH STUMPERS

1. A bank teller gets a check for $457.90. The customer wants to deposit $239.00 in savings and would like $141.90 in checking. They would like the rest in cash. The customer would like to have the cash in tens, 2 fives, and at least 7 ones. How much money do you owe the customer and how many bills of each increment would you give to the customer?

   • How much money to the customer? _____

   • How many tens? _____

   • How many fives? _____

   • How many ones? _____

2. A farmer is going to plant a large field of corn, beans, and squash. He would like to have 25 rows of each vegetable. It takes about 240 seeds of corn to fill up one row, 190 seeds of beans to fill up one row, and 206 seeds of squash to fill up each row. Seeds come in bags of 1000. How many bags of each would the farmer need to buy?

   • How many bags of corn? _____

   • How many bags of beans? _____

   • How many bags of squash? _____

3. A news reporter takes about 230 pictures per month. The supervisor has to make a yearly budget for film. A 36 roll of film costs $4.59. A 24 rolls of film costs $3.56.

   • How many rolls need to be bought of the 24 roll of film for the year? _____

   • What is the cost of buying enough of this film? _____

   • How many rolls of the 36 rolls of film would need to be bought? _____

   • What is the cost of buying enough of this film? _____

   • Which number roll of film is the best buy, 24 or 36? _____

   • How much money will we save by buying the least expensive film? _____

4. A food services manager at a school cafeteria must feed 500 children per day. If 239 children eat breakfast every day and 500 children eat lunch every day and each of these children must get one milk carton at every meal, how many cartons of milk should be ordered for one week?

   _____

5. If 298 children per day like to drink chocolate milk, 43 children per day like to drink strawberry milk, and the rest like to drink white milk, how many cartons of each kind of milk should be bought for the week? The total number of children who eat breakfast and lunch is 739.

   _____

CAREER MATH STUMPERS

Answer Key for page 98

1. 77,6 tens, 2 fives, 7 ones
2. corn-6, beans-5, squash-6
3. rolls-10, cost $35.60, rolls of 35mm-7, film cost - $32.15, best-36 roll, saved-$3.47
4. 3695 cartons
5. 1490 chocolate, 215 strawberry, 1990 white milk

EASY MATH STOMPERS

Answer Key for page 100

1. needs 2 more
2. 6 roses, 6 carnations
3. 6 shoes
4. 9 minutes
5. cut in half
6. 28 patients
7. 20 sandwiches
8. 6 men

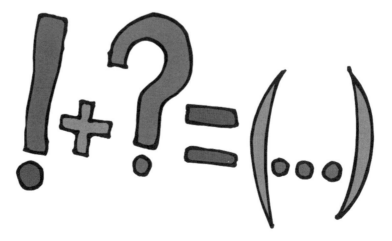

EASY MATH STUMPERS

1. A brick mason has 3 bricks and needs 5 bricks to finish the wall. How many bricks does the brick mason need to be able to finish the wall?

2. The florist is going to fix a vase of flowers for 3 people. She would like to put 2 roses and 2 carnations in each vase. How many roses and carnations will she need to order?

3. A salesperson at a store sold 2 pairs of shoes each day on Monday, Wednesday, and Friday. How many pairs of shoes did the salesperson sell for the week?

4. A singer needs to sing 3 songs at a wedding. Each song lasts for 3 minutes. The bride does not want the songs to last over 10 minutes. How long will the songs last?

5. A bakery has 10 cookies left. 20 children walk in the store and each wants a cookie. What can the baker do so that everybody can have one cookie?

6. A doctor asks the receptionist to tell him how many patients he has seen today. The receptionist looks at the schedule to find this out.
   - From 8 - 10 am he saw 5 patients.
   - From 10-12 am he saw 8 patients.
   - From 12-1 PM he ate lunch.
   - From 1-3 PM he saw 7 patients
   - From 3-5 PM he saw 8 patients.   How many patients did the doctor see?_____

7. A caterer wants to serve 10 people. How many sandwiches does she need to fix if everyone eats 2 sandwiches?

8. The space shuttle has room for 8 people. Only 2 ladies are going on the mission. How many men can go?

Character Education

Character Education

Building good character is necessary for children to become all they can in a world that is increasingly complex and often confusing. Our culture displays many conflicting values, and it is important for children to examine these core values and develop those traits that are positive in their lives. Developing these traits of integrity, honesty, respectfulness, responsibility, and compassion are necessary for developing good citizens, strong families, excellent leaders, and productive workers. In fact, the survival of our society depends on a level of the mutual trust of human beings to do what is basically right in any given situation. Character education emphasizes these traits and encourages students to develop positive traits to use in their daily lives.

Drug abuse, alcohol abuse, delinquency, and other negative behaviors all result from the inability to make wise decisions in difficult situations. The activities in this chapter examine common everyday situations where children are forced to make difficult decisions and the strategies listed in the activities encourage them to make smart choices. The games are fun and non-threatening and emphasize the importance of positive character traits in many situations. The goal is to help children learn and develop positive traits that will help them to be more compassionate about others and better equipped to reach their personal goals.

STEP AND STOMP

Grade Level: 2nd - Middle School

Time: 30 minutes

Purpose: To identify character traits that are necessary to be used in life situations

Materials Needed: Step and stomp floor board, a balloon that is blown up and tied, Step and Stomp Situation Question Cards (chart or reproduced and cut out), character trait chart

Object: To earn the most points by correctly guessing the character traits necessary for certain real life situations and then correctly spelling the character traits within a time limit

Procedures:

1. Develop a large game board that consists of the letters of the alphabet arranged in alphabetical order. This can be made on a large piece of bulletin board paper where you can simply write the letters or tape small pieces of colorful construction paper to the paper. See example below:

    A B C D E F G H I J
    K L M N O P Q R S
    T U V W X Y Z

2. Divide the students into two teams.

3. Review several examples of character words. Explain that students may refer to the chart when answering situation questions.

4. Choose a student to begin the game by asking the student a character situation question. You may either ask a student a question from the chart or cut out and reproduce the situation game cards and allow students to choose a card. Explain that each situation card describes a scenario that indicates a need for a particular character trait that can be used in that situation.

5. If the student is able to come up with the character trait, he/she is given thirty seconds to step and stomp (easily) on the letters on the character board in order to spell the trait he/she has chosen. (Feel free to vary the time limit for varying levels of student ability.) In order to be successful, the student must successfully step on all of the letters of the word within the allotted time period.

6. If the student is successful, give the team an opportunity to win points by playing the balloon game. Ask the stepping student to choose two other teammates and ask these three students to join hands to complete a circle. Give the students thirty seconds to see how many times they can keep the balloon in the air without the balloon dropping to the floor or without them dropping hands. Students may use their hands, heads, knees, etc. and may move around as necessary to keep the balloon in the air. Three things may end the game: (1) The time limit is over. (2) Someone drops hands in the circle. (3) The balloon hits the floor. Count the number of times the balloon was batted in the air, and use this number as the team's score for that round.

7. Continue as time allows and award the winning team as the team that has collected the most points.

FOLLOW-UP:

This activity uses tactile learning to emphasize the strategies students are using. Just as it is important for students to spell the strategies quickly, it is important in life to think of good character strategies and implement them quickly in difficult situations. The balloon activity is a cooperative activity that teaches working together to get points for the team. Therefore, cooperation skills are also covered as a part of the character education game.

STEP AND STOMP SITUATION QUESTIONS

Answers correspond to the chart so that the answer to question number one is character trait number one.

1. You are playing baseball with your friend, and your ball accidentally breaks a pot on your neighbor's porch. What trait is needed, and what should you do?

2. You've always been best friends with someone who's not very popular in class. The most popular guy in class asks you to drop your old best friend because he is not "cool." What trait is needed, and what should you do?

3. Your group is trying to work together to finish a project. One person keeps putting his/her head down and goofing off, and the group can't get their project finished. What trait is needed, and what should this student do?

4. An adult asks you to sit down and complete an assignment. You'd rather tell the adult in a grumpy voice that you don't want to. But you don't because……… What trait is needed and what should you do?

5. Mr. Johnson asks if you would like to participate in the spelling contest. You reply, "No, thank you Mr. Johnson, but thanks for asking." This is called _____ behavior.

6. A friend asks you if you would like to take a sip of his parent's stash of alcohol. All of your friends take a sip. What trait is needed, and what should you do?

7. You want to be sure you are successful so you always bring in your reading assignments to class even if your parents don't check on you. This is called _____ behavior.

8. You help around the house, help your grandmother mow her grass, earn your allowance by doing your chores, always do your homework, always clean your room, and always do your schoolwork. This person could be referred to as a _____.

9. When you told your friend that you'd meet them at the movies at 5:00, you were there. When you told your friend that you'd repay the lunch money you borrowed, you repaid the money the next day. You are called a _____ person when you always do what you say you'll do.

10. Your friend tells you a secret that is not harmful and asks you not to tell. Although you might want to tell, you never do. Your friend is glad because she thinks of you as a _____ person who always keeps her promises.

11. There is a student in your class who always eats alone. Sometimes people make fun of him. You decide to be a friend and eat with this person. This is called being _____.

12. You get a new kitten at home. Your brother torments the kitten by playing roughly with her. Your mom wants you to be a different way with the cat. What trait is needed, and what should you do?

13. You are someone who is always there, true to your friends, keeps your promises, doesn't do things to destroy friendships, and is very dependable. This is called being _____.

14. You give your mom a hug, you make a gift for your aunt because she helped you with your homework, you do nice things for your friends, and you tell your dad you appreciate him. This behavior is called _____.

15. Someone keeps picking on you, and you are so angry. You want to punch them some time to make them stop, but you don't because you have _____ which makes you think twice before acting.

16. When other people are trying to start fights and you try to help them to get along without fighting, you are helping by having a _____ personality.

17. You're trying to help your friend with his/her math, but he/she just can't get it. It's easy for you, but you don't act frustrated and you keep helping until your friend gets the answer. This is called having _____.

18. You have a positive, happy outlook and try to see the bright side of things. This is called being _____.

19. Your friend is negative all the time about school, about parents, about sports, and about people. You try to think of good things about school, parents, sports, and people. You are exhibiting the opposite of negative behavior which is called having _____ behavior.

20. When a new student comes to your class, no one talks to the student. The student looks sad. What trait is needed, and what do you do?

21. Someone is feeling sad because something happened to him/her. He/she puts his/her head down and looks as if crying. He/she forgot the homework. It sounds as if this person needs a friend to share some _____ to help that person feel better.

22. Someone has to go to the hospital for surgery, but the family can't pay the bills. Your school is going to have a fund-raiser to help them out. Hopefully, a lot of people will have this character trait so that the family can get help. What is the trait?

23. You have two pencils, someone else has none. What trait is needed and what should you do?

24. Someone acts as if his/her schoolwork doesn't matter, the family doesn't matter, and friends don't matter. This character trait doesn't help. What trait is needed to show that family, friends, and schoolwork matter a lot?

STEP AND STOMP SITUATION QUESTION CARDS

1.
You are playing baseball with your friend, and your ball accidentally breaks a pot on your neighbor's porch. What trait is needed, and what should you do?

2.
You've always been best friends with someone who's not very popular in class. The most popular guy in class asks you to drop your old best friend because he is not "cool." What trait is needed, and what should you do?

3.
Your group is trying to work together to finish a project. One person keeps putting his/her head down and goofing off, and the group can't get their project finished. What trait is needed, and what should this student do?

4.
An adult asks you to sit down and complete an assignment. You'd rather tell the adult in a grumpy voice that you don't want to. But you don't because_____ What trait is needed and what should you do?

5.
Mr. Johnson asks if you would like to participate in the spelling contest. You reply, "No, thank you Mr. Johnson, but thanks for asking." This is called _____ behavior.

6.
A friend asks you if you would like to take a sip of his parent's stash of alcohol. All of your friends take a sip. What trait is needed, and what should you do?

STEP AND STOMP SITUATION QUESTION CARDS

7.
You want to be sure you are successful so you always bring in your reading assignments to class even if your parents don't check on you. This is called

_____

behavior.

8.
You help around the house, help your grandmother mow her grass, earn your allowance by doing your chores, always do your homework, always clean your room, and always do your schoolwork. This person could be referred to as a

_____

person.

9.
When you told your friend that you'd meet them at the movies at 5:00, you were there. When you told your friend that you'd repay the lunch money you borrowed, you repaid the money the next day. You are called a

_____ person

when you always do what you say you'll do.

10.
Your friend tells you a secret that is not harmful and asks you not to tell. Although you might want to tell, you never do. Your friend is glad because she thinks of you as a _____ person who always keeps her promises.

11.
There is a student in your class who always eats alone. Sometimes people make fun of him. You decide to be a friend and eat with this person. This is called being _____.

12.
You get a new kitten at home. Your brother torments the kitten by playing roughly with her. Your mom wants you to act in a nicer way with the cat. What trait is needed, and what should you do?

STEP AND STOMP SITUATION QUESTION CARDS

13.
You are someone who is always there, true to your friends, keeps your promises, doesn't do things to destroy friendships, and is very dependable. This is called being

_____.

14.
You give your mom a hug, you make a gift for your aunt because she helped you with your homework, you do nice things for your friends, and you tell your dad you appreciate him. This behavior is called being

_____.

15.
Someone keeps picking on you, and you are so angry. You want to punch them some time to make them stop, but you don't because you have _____ which makes you think twice before acting.

16.
When other people are trying to start fights and you try to help them to get along without fighting, you are helping by having a

_____
personality.

17.
You're trying to help your friend with his/her math, but he/she just can't get it. It's easy for you, but you don't act frustrated and you keep helping until your friend gets the answer. This is called having

_____.

18.
You have a positive, happy outlook and try to see the bright side of things. This is called being

_____.

STEP AND STOMP SITUATION QUESTION CARDS

19.
Your friend is negative all the time about school, about parents, about sports, and about people. You try to think of good things about school, parents, sports, and people. You are exhibiting the opposite of negative behavior which is called having _____ behavior.

20.
When a new student comes to your class, no one talks to the student. The student looks sad. What trait is needed, and what do you do?

21.
Someone is feeling sad because something happened to him/her. He/she puts his/her head down and looks as if he/she is crying. He/she forgot the homework. It sounds as if this person needs a friend to share some_____ words to help that person feel better.

22.
Someone has to go to the hospital for surgery, but the family can't pay the bills. Your school is going to have a fundraiser to help them out. Hopefully, a lot of people will have this character trait so that the family can get help. What is the trait?

23.
You have two pencils, someone else has none. What trait is needed and what should you do?

24.
Someone acts as if his/her schoolwork doesn't matter, the family doesn't matter, and friends don't matter. This character trait doesn't help. What trait is needed to show that family, friends, and schoolwork matter a lot?

STEP AND STOMP CHARACTER TRAITS

1.	Honest
2.	Loyalty
3.	Cooperative
4.	Respect
5.	Polite
6.	Courage
7.	Responsible
8.	Hard worker
9.	Dependable
10.	Trustworthy
11.	Kind
12.	Gentleness
13.	Faithful
14.	Love
15.	Self control
16.	Peaceful
17.	Patience
18.	Joyful
19.	Positive
20.	Friendliness
21.	Encouragement
22.	Unselfishness
23.	Sharing
24.	Caring

Answer Key

STEP AND STOMP CHARACTER TRAITS

Hard worker
Dependable
Friendliness
Encouragement
Trustworthy
Honesty
Unselfishness
Sharing
Caring
Loyalty
Self control
Peaceful
Cooperation
Respect
Polite
Courage
Gentleness
Faithful
Love
Responsible
Kind
Patience
Joyful
Positive

TRAPPED

Grade Level: 2nd - Middle School

Time: 30 minutes

Purpose: To demonstrate that negative behaviors trap us into ineffective habits that will hinder our success

Object: To be the team that gets the most points by choosing positive cards and having the shortest amount of yarn wrapped around them. To gain points by being the first team to successfully complete the challenge task.

Materials Needed: 2 spools of yarn, game cards (reproduced and cut out), basket for the cards, Hershey kisses (or other small piece of candy that requires a little bit of effort to unwrap), 2 pieces of paper and 2 pencils

Procedures:

1. Divide the class into two teams.

2. Ask for one volunteer per team to come to the front of the room to play the first round of the game. Before beginning the game, explain that the game will involve having yarn loosely wrapped around his/her waist and arms at the side. Check to make sure that the chosen volunteers do not mind having yarn wound around them. If this is acceptable, ask each volunteer to hold the end of one spool of yarn.

3. Begin by asking another team member of one team to draw a character situation card. If the situation card demonstrates a positive character trait, award the team five points. If the situation card demonstrates a negative character trait, award the team zero points. However, when the volunteer's team draws the negative character cards, wrap the yarn loosely around the person the number of times specified on the card. For example, if the card has the number three written on it, gently wrap the yarn three full times around the waist and arms of the volunteer person.

4. Play in round one will consist of five turns for each team. After each person draws a card, ask teams to discuss whether the situation presented on the card was a positive or negative character trait.

5. Complete one of two actions each time a card is drawn.
    (1) Award points for the positive character choices.
    (2) Wrap yarn around the player for the negative card choices.

    Consider the following as you are wrapping yarn around students:
    • Always be sure the student is comfortable with this activity.
    • Always be sure the yarn is loose enough for the student to feel comfortable, but tight enough so that it does not continually fall off.
    • Begin by wrapping the yarn around the waist and outside of the arms to allow less arm

movement. This will confine the arms a little more. (Yarn is still on outside of arms.)
- Eventually try to wrap a little yarn around the legs of the volunteer.

The purpose of this activity is to demonstrate how negative choices give you fewer and fewer choices in life. Therefore, you want the volunteer to have fewer choices in the final challenge.

6. Complete the following challenge once you have drawn five cards per team. At this point, hopefully one player will have a little more yarn wrapped around themselves to make this challenge a little more difficult.
   - Establish a starting point.
   - Challenge the two students to race to a location which is about ten feet away, unwrap a Hershey's kiss, write their name on the board or a piece of paper, and walk back to the starting line.
   - Award the team 25 points for the winner of this challenge.
   - Add the 25 points to any previous points given for the positive character cards.

7. Scoring example:
   - Team one got 4 positive character cards for 20 points.
   - Team one won the challenge because he/she was not very wrapped up. Team one gets 20 points for the cards plus 25 points for winning the challenge for a total of 45 points.
   - Team two got 1 positive character card for 5 points.
   - Team two did not win the challenge and ends up with a total of 5 points.

8. Continue the game as time allows by choosing new team members to come to the front to complete round two.

FOLLOW-UP:

Ask students the following questions after playing the game.

1. What happened when you got too many negative cards?
2. How did that affect you being able to win the challenge?
3. To the players that may have gotten really wrapped up: Did the yarn make you feel really trapped? To the class: Do you think that some people feel really trapped because of decisions they've made? What about people in jail?
4. Do you ever see famous people or people on TV who feel trapped because of their decisions?
5. What happened when you got a lot of positive cards?
6. How did that affect your being able to win the challenge?
7. In real life, what happens when you do a lot of negative things?
8. What kind of trouble do you get into?
9. Does it affect your success in school? Why?
10. Does it affect your success in sports, at home, or with your family?
11. Does it affect your ability to be successful in life?
12. Are you successful if you are doing good things and making good decision? Why?
13. Do negative choices affect your success in school, sports, home, and with your family?
14. What can we learn about decision making from this game?

114

© YouthLight, Inc.

TRAPPED CHARACTER CARDS

You don't know how to do your work. You ask the teacher.	**You don't know how to do your work, you copy off someone's paper.** 3 points	**You don't like someone because the color of his or her skin is different from yours.** 4 points
You try to get to know other people even if they're different from you.	**You ask new friends questions to try to get to know them.**	**You try to sit with the new transfer student who doesn't know anyone in the lunch room.**
You make up a story and tell everyone that the new transfer student has failed his/her grade before. It's not true. 3 points	**You tease people almost every day.** 4 points	**You pull people's hair.** 2 points

TRAPPED CHARACTER CARDS

You give compliments to others.	**You try to have a good attitude most every day.**	**You are polite to the teacher.**
You do not talk back to adults.	**You always talk back to adults.** 4 points	**You bully other students.** 5 points
Even if you're upset, you try to peacefully work out your problems.	**You turn in your homework each day.**	**You study every night to make sure you do your best in school.**

TRAPPED CHARACTER CARDS

You never turn in your homework. 6 points	You don't really care if your work is neat. Most days you only do one thing on the page. 3 points	You get in fights after school. 6 points
You do your chores at home.	You offer to help the teacher clean up.	After you've finished your work, you offer to help others.
You walk away from gossip.	You always talk about your friends. 4 points	You always start rumors about people who you don't like. 4 points

TRAPPED CHARACTER CARDS

You love to roll your eyes when you don't like something. 5 points	**You believe the teacher should just give you a good grade. You think there is no reason to work hard to achieve a good grade.** 3 points	**You have a negative attitude.** 6 points
You have a positive attitude.	**You help others.**	**You are honest.**
You are kind.	**You are dishonest.** 7 points	**You are unkind to others.** 3 points

ROLLER COASTER

Grade Level: K - 5th

Time: 30 minutes

Materials Needed: Good and Poor Character List

Purpose: To recognize good & poor character traits

Object: To jump up first when hearing a good character trait described

Procedures:

1. Discuss good character qualities such as honesty, responsibility, respect, patience, etc.

2. Explain that the lesson is about going on a Roller Coaster of good and poor character traits.

3. Choose three students to come to the front of the room. They must squat down, ready to jump up if they hear good character traits described, but remain down if poor character traits are described. The first one who jumps up at a good character description is the winner.

4. Choose two more challengers to come up front to begin another round of Roller Coaster.

5. Retire the winner after three wins to later come back up for an all winners Roller Coaster competition. Continue on with three new students and another round when the winner retires.

FOLLOW-UP:

Bring out the favorite good character quality and the most difficult one to achieve. Why is it important to work on good character? How is building good character similar to being on a Roller Coaster?

GOOD CHARACTER TRAITS:

Loyal

Patient

Cooperative

Obedient

Prompt

Attentive

Clean

Positive

Dependable

Responsible

Kind

Fair

Good Sport

Polite

Neat

Caring

Hard working

Respectful

Thankful

Honest

POOR CHARACTER TRAITS:

Stubborn

Disobedient

Impatient

Negative

Quitter

Messy

Mean

Dirty

Lazy

Unappreciative

Late

Thoughtless

Rude

Bad sport

Hostile

Irresponsible

Dishonest

HOT DOG

Grade Level: 2nd - 5th

Time: 30 minutes

Materials Needed: Hot Dog Cards

Purpose: To recognize good character traits

Object: To make a Hot Dog Card match

Procedures:

1. Review examples of good character traits that the class has discussed in previous lessons.

2. Explain that in the activity of Hot Dog, everyone is trying to make a Hot Dog match by pairing up the name of a good character trait with an example or definition of that trait.

3. Distribute one card to each student from two mixed decks of cards that are two different colors. One color gives the name of the good character trait, and the other colored card gives a definition or example of that trait. Be sure you only distribute matching cards which both have a matching letter. Mix up the colors together after you check that they all have matches.

4. Begin with any volunteer to read his/her card. It does not matter whether the person has the naming trait card or the describing trait card.

5. Tell the students to listen to the reading of each card and to raise their hand if their card matches the one being read. That makes a Hot Dog, and the two winners may write their names on the board under the title of Hot Dog.

6. Give the two winners two new matching cards, which they can then trade with a friend at the same time as everyone else also trades cards with someone near them.

7. Continue as before by calling on a volunteer to read aloud his/her card and having others respond by raising their hand if there is a match.

FOLLOW-UP:

Determine what helped students to make a match. Share the examples of good character that they see in others.

HOT DOG CARDS

Directions: Make copies of cards in two different colors.

Answer Key:

OBEDIENT	To do what the authority asks
POSITIVE	To never think of quitting
CARING	To be interested in others
PATIENT	To be able to wait your turn
COOPERATIVE	To listen to others' ideas & To work well with others
GOOD SPORT	To not complain about losing
LOYAL	To stick up for a friend
KIND	To be nice to others
DEPENDABLE	To try to do what you say you will do
FORGIVING	To accept someone's apology & not seek revenge
POLITE	To use good manners
RESPECTFUL	To treat others the way you would like to be treated

HOT DOG TRAIT CARDS

Obedient	Positive	Caring
Patient	Cooperative	Good Sport

HOT DOG TRAIT CARDS

Loyal	**Kind**	**Dependable**
Forgiving	**Polite**	**Respectful**

HOT DOG DEFINITION CARDS

To do what the authority asks	**To never think of quitting**	**To be interested in others**
To be able to wait your turn	**To listen to others' ideas & to work well with others**	**To not complain about losing**

HOT DOG DEFINITION CARDS

To stick up for a friend	To be nice to others	To try to do what you say you will do
To accept someone's apology & not seek revenge	To use good manners	To treat others the way you would like to be treated

BUNGIE JUMP

Grade Level: 2nd - 5th

Time: 30 minutes

Materials Needed: Bungie Cards

Purpose: To recognize and value good citizenship

Object: To hop toward someone with a good citizenship Bungie Card

Procedures:

1. Discuss what it means to have good citizenship. Bring out examples such as helping others, obeying laws or rules, taking care of yourself, being safe, being healthy, etc.

2. Choose five students to come to the front of the class. Give each one a Bungie Jump card to take turns reading aloud.

3. Choose two students to go to the back of the room or let one student choose someone to challenge. After the five students each read their cards aloud, ask the two students in the back of the room to start hopping on one foot toward at least one of the students who read a good citizenship example. The one who gets to the correct destination first is the Bungie Jumper Champion.

4. Start the next round in the same way by having two new players at the back of the room and five new ones at the front with new cards to read.

FOLLOW-UP:

Ask which good citizenship example describes something that you personally try to do, and why do you think that is important?

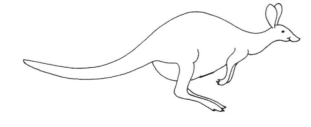

BUNGIE CARDS

GOOD CITIZENSHIP **Using appropriate language** 	GOOD CITIZENSHIP **Listening to others**	POOR CITIZENSHIP **Lying to others**
POOR CITIZENSHIP **Not doing what you are asked to do** 	GOOD CITIZENSHIP **Telling the truth** 	POOR CITIZENSHIP **Ignoring Others**
GOOD CITIZENSHIP **Making good choices** 	POOR CITIZENSHIP **Not caring about the needs of others** 	GOOD CITIZENSHIP **Treating others the way that you want to be treated**

BUNGIE CARDS

GOOD CITIZENSHIP	GOOD CITIZENSHIP	POOR CITIZENSHIP
Being on time	**Being careful with animals**	**Being late**
POOR CITIZENSHIP	GOOD CITIZENSHIP	POOR CITIZENSHIP
Not following directions	**Being patient**	**Being unsafe**
GOOD CITIZENSHIP	POOR CITIZENSHIP	GOOD CITIZENSHIP
Thinking of the needs of others	**Being messy and dirty**	**Accepting responsibility for what you do**

BUNGIE CARDS

POOR CITIZENSHIP	GOOD CITIZENSHIP	POOR CITIZENSHIP
Hurting animals	**Obeying rules**	**Staying angry**
POOR CITIZENSHIP	GOOD CITIZENSHIP	POOR CITIZENSHIP
Not obeying	**Accepting authority**	**Making poor choices**
GOOD CITIZENSHIP	POOR CITIZENSHIP	POOR CITIZENSHIP
Taking turns	**Not being fair**	**Disrespecting the rights of others**

BUNGIE CARDS

GOOD CITIZENSHIP	GOOD CITIZENSHIP	POOR CITIZENSHIP
Keeping safe	**Respecting the rights of others**	**Not Taking turns**
POOR CITIZENSHIP	GOOD CITIZENSHIP	POOR CITIZENSHIP
To only have your way	**Following directions**	**Being mean to others**
GOOD CITIZENSHIP	POOR CITIZENSHIP	POOR CITIZENSHIP
Staying calm and not angry	**Being lazy and not working**	**Having bad manners**

RACE TO THE TOP

Grade Level: 2nd - Middle School

Time: 30 minutes

Purpose: To teach children the importance of developing positive character traits.
To differentiate between positive and negative character traits.

Object: To collect the most points and to reach the top of the mountain before the other team

Materials Needed: Poster board, yarn, cut out figures, character cards reproduced and cut out.

PROCEDURES:

1. Make the game board by following the directions listed below:
   - Obtain a piece of poster board or other type of stiff paper.
   - Fold the paper into thirds. The middle section should be the largest. The purpose of this folding pattern is so that the paper can stand alone on a table while you play the game.
   - Draw the following picture on the middle section.

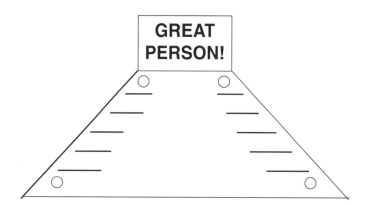

   - Place an equal number of marks on each side as represented above. You may put 5 marks if you want the rounds to go faster or 7 or 8 if you want the rounds to go a little slower.
   - Hole punch the small areas (two on each side) as represented by the circles on the diagram above.
   - Cut out two pieces of yarn (one for each side of the hill). Make sure each piece of yarn is long enough to go through the two holes on the side of the board and be tied together at the back. Do not put the yarn through the holes and tie it yet.
   - Cut out the two figures. Hole punch two small holes - one in the top of the figure and one in the bottom of the figure.
   - Put the yarn through the figures by first threading it through the bottom of the figure with the yarn facing the back of the figure and then back through the top of the figure with the yarn coming through to the front.

- Now place the yarn with the figure attached to it on the game board and thread both ends of the yarn through the holes at the bottom and top of the hill. The figure will now be on the front of the board. Tie the yarn at the back of the board.
- You should now be able to move the figure up and down the game board by pulling the yarn from the back of the game board.
- Repeat the procedure on the other side.

2. Place the character cards into a basket.

3. Divide the class into two teams.

4. Explain that the object of the game is to earn points by being the first team to reach the top. The top is signified by a block with the words "great person" written on them. You may substitute other words like college, careers, great character, etc.

5. Play the game by choosing one volunteer from each team to come up to the front of the room.

6. Ask each player to choose a character card. Each card will have a phrase written on it that will signify a positive or negative character trait. If the trait is a positive trait, allow the team to move their figure one notch on the climb. If the trait represents a negative trait, do not allow the person to move their figure.

7. Award the team that reaches the top first 10 points. After one team has reached the top, move both figures down to the bottom of the hill and begin the game again.

8. Continue play as time allows.

FOLLOW-UP:

Ask students the following questions:
1. Do you think positive character traits really do help you get to the top?
2. Do negative traits ever help anyone get to the top? Why or why not?
3. What character traits can you think of that would help you do better in school?
4. What character traits would hold you back in school?
5. What character traits will you need to go to college?
6. What character traits could keep you from college?
7. What character traits do your friends like? Dislike?

Discuss the importance of positive character traits in being successful in every area of life and how these aid you in reaching your goals. You may even want to discuss historical or literary characters and how character traits helped or hindered their success or goals. You may also discuss various careers like postal workers, police officers, teachers, doctors, airplane pilots, etc. and the importance of having positive traits. Discuss what happens when people are dishonest or do illegal things and the consequences of such actions.

CUT OUT FIGURES

CHARACTER CARDS

You do all your work in school.	**You cheat on your papers.**	**You gossip about your friends.**
You sometimes buy a little gift for your friend when he/she is sad.	**You are a bully.**	**You never do your homework.**
You study every night.	**You are polite to adults.**	**You steal every chance that you get.**

CHARACTER CARDS

You never take a bath. 😊☹️	**You stand up for what is right.** 😊☹️	**You make fun of people.** 😊☹️
You bully people. 😊☹️	**You try to be kind to others.** 😊☹️	**You tell lies most of the time.** 😊☹️
You are honest. 😊☹️	**You start smoking.** 😊☹️	**You start drinking.** 😊☹️

CHARACTER CARDS

You try to eat healthy.	**You exercise.**	**You help people.**
You help your parents.	**You always talk back to your parents.**	**You make fun of people who are different from you.**
You don't join in when others are making fun of someone.	**You stick up for others who are being bullied.**	**You pay attention in class.**

CHARACTER BINGO

Grade Level: 2nd - Middle School

Purpose: To identify appropriate and inappropriate character traits

Materials Needed: Blank bingo cards (reproduced for students) character cards, small pieces of construction paper to cover answers

Object: To be the first person to get a bingo either horizontally, vertically, or any other way you call

Procedures:

1. Give each student a bingo board.

2. Give students a paper with all character traits listed, or read out the list of all character traits. Ask students to randomly write the character traits on their bingo board. (Allowing the students to write the answers, assures that all cards are different and students do not all get bingo at the same time.)

3. Cut out and distribute small pieces of paper. The paper should be small enough to fit over the bingo boxes.

4. Place the character cards that you have reproduced and cut out in a small basket.

5. Explain to students the kind of bingo you are looking for in the first win. (straight line, four corners, etc.)

6. Begin the game by calling up a student to choose a character card. This card will represent either a positive or negative character trait. Ask the student or the class to determine if this is a positive or negative trait.

7. If the trait is a positive trait, ask the class if they can remember a time they personally demonstrated this particular trait. Ask the student to share briefly about this person and how he/she demonstrated the trait.

8. Spend time discussing each character trait as it is called out emphasizing why it is or is not appropriate

9. Continue playing as time allows. You may call for one bingo and start over or call for several different kinds of bingo's before you start over.

FOLLOW UP:

Character traits are often choices that we make just as we choose the cards in the basket. Ask the following questions:

1. Is it easier to choose positive character traits or negative character traits?

2. Does it usually depend on the people you are around?

3. Is it important to be around people you think are positive influences?

4. What if there are a lot of negative influences in your neighborhood?

5. Do you think families have a lot to do with your choices?

6. Do your parents have all the responsibility for all the choices you make?

7. How easy is it to change a negative character trait once you have it?

8. Do people respect you more for positive or for negative character traits?

CHARACTER TRAIT CARDS

BINGO	BINGO	BINGO
Honesty	**Loyalty**	**Caring**
BINGO **Cheating**	**FREE SPACE**	BINGO **Stealing**
BINGO **Kindness**	BINGO **Citizenship**	BINGO **Bullying**

CHARACTER TRAIT CARDS

BINGO	BINGO	BINGO
Teasing	**Hard working**	**Making fun of others**
BINGO **Gentleness**	**FREE SPACE**	BINGO **Understanding**
BINGO **Yelling**	BINGO **Screaming**	BINGO **Criticizing**

CHARACTER TRAIT CARDS

BINGO **Being disrespectful**	BINGO **Having a bad attitude**	BINGO **Joyfulness**
BINGO **Hateful**	**FREE SPACE**	BINGO **Loving**
BINGO **Being patient**	BINGO **Having self-control**	BINGO **Persevering**

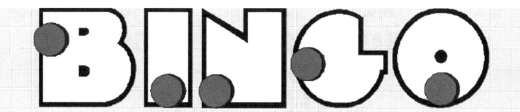

		FREE SPACE		

GO FIGURE
CHARACTER PUZZLE

Grade Level: 3rd - Middle School

Time: 15 minutes per puzzle

Purpose: To teach children lessons on character education

Materials Needed: Copies of puzzles for everyone

Object: To complete the puzzle and discover the answer

Procedures:

1. Hand out the puzzles to the class.

2. Ask the students to complete the puzzles and discover the secret messages hidden within the puzzles.

3. Share with the class the answers and discuss what the puzzle actually means.

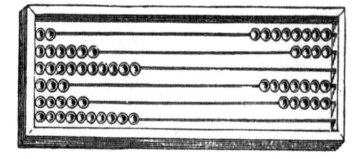

GO FIGURE CHARACTER PUZZLE

Calculate the answers to all of the math problems. Record these answers in the answer column. After you have completed writing the answers, then place the answers in numeric order ranging from 1 through 17 beginning with the lowest numeric value and continuing to the highest numeric value. Record these numbers in the order column. Write the words in a sentence in the same order as indicated by the numbers 1 - 17 to discover the hidden message.

For example:

PROBLEM	ANSWER	ORDER	WORDS
25 + 25 =	50	2	Like
2 x 2 =	4	1	We
10 x 7 =	70	3	Challenges

Sentence: We like challenges.

PROBLEM	ANSWER	ORDER	WORDS
59 - 38 =			To
6 x 4 =			Discover
7 x 5 =			Others
101 - 61 =			We
40 - 8 =			In
10 + 4 =			When
25 - 6 =			Seek
2 x 8 =			We
3 x 10 =			Best
50 / 2 =			The
11 x 4 =			Bring
12 x 5 =			Best
9 x 5 =			Out
33 x 3 =			Ourselves
150 / 2 =			In
200 - 150 =			The
500 / 5 =			William Ward

GO FIGURE CHARACTER PUZZLE
Answer Key

Calculate the answers to all of the math problems. Record these answers in the answer column. After you have completed writing the answers, then place the answers in numeric order ranging from 1 through 17 beginning with the lowest numeric value and continuing to the highest numeric value. Record these numbers in the order column. Write the words in a sentence in the same order as indicated by the numbers 1 - 17 to discover the hidden message. (Note: The following numerical denotation implies division. Example: 10/2 means 10 divided by 2)

For example:

PROBLEM	ANSWER	ORDER	WORDS
25 + 25 =	50	2	Like
2 x 2 =	4	1	We
10 x 7 =	70	3	Challenges

Sentence: We like challenges.

Answer Key

PROBLEM	ANSWER	ORDER	WORDS
59 -3 8 =	21	4	To
6 x 4 =	24	5	Discover
7 x 5 =	35	9	Others
101 - 61 =	40	10	We
40 - 8 =	32	8	In
10 + 4 =	14	1	When
25 - 6 =	19	3	Seek
2 x 8 =	16	2	We
3 x 10 =	30	7	Best
50 / 2 =	25	6	The
11 x 4 =	44	11	Bring
12 x 5 =	60	14	Best
9 x 5 =	45	12	Out
33 x 3 =	99	16	Ourselves
150 / 2 =	75	15	In
200 - 150 =	50	13	The
500 / 5 =	100	17	William Ward

PUZZLE KEY:
When we seek to bring out the best in others, we bring out the best in ourselves.

WHICH WAY DO WE GO?
CHARACTER PUZZLE

Grade Level: 3rd - Middle School

Time: 15 minutes per puzzle

Purpose: To teach children lessons on character education

Materials Needed: Copies of puzzles for everyone

Object: To complete the puzzle and discover the answer

Procedures:

1. Hand out the puzzles to the class.

2. Ask the students to complete the puzzles and discover the secret messages hidden within the puzzles.

    Example:

X	O →	D
Y	O ↑	Z
G ↗	P	M

G   O   O   D
 ↗   ↑   →

3. Share with the class the answers and discuss what the puzzle actually means.

FOLLOW-UP:
1. What does this statement mean?
2. How do you think we can take advantage of other people?
3. Is telling jokes about other people considered taking advantage?
4. Is laughing at someone's clothes taking advantage?
5. Is trying to tell someone a lie to get someone to do something for you taking advantage?
6. What are some things that you can do that are nice for others who may be having a difficult time? For example, what could you do for someone…..
   • From a different country
   • Who can't learn as fast as you can
   • Who doesn't have the nicest clothes in the class
   • Who eats alone
   • Who doesn't have school supplies
   • Who forgot their lunch money
7. Try to think of a time this week when you can be nice to someone who needs a friend.

WHICH WAY DO WE GO?

DIRECTION SECTION:

Beginning with the "n" in the lower left corner, follow the directional arrows to discover the next letter. Write the letters in the blanks provided to discover a hidden message.

F	O	A	T	O	I	U	Y
A	F	G	N	R	W	D	F
N	O	E	A	D	A	K	J
Y	N	E	V	T	E	K	A
X	C	V	A	N	B	T	N
C	E	R	B	C	T	O	X
W	V	B	T	E	Y	Q	Z
V	E	M	T	R	B	V	C
N	J	G	H	H	J	K	L

N ___ ___ ___ ___ ___   Y ___ ___ ___ ___   K ___ ___ ___ ___
↗ ↗ ↑ ↑ →   ↘ ↘ ↗ ↑ →   ↑ ↗ ← ←

T ___ ___ ___ ___ ___ ___ O ___ ___ ___
↑ ← ↗ ↑ ↑ ↑ ← ↓ ↓ ← ↑

Y ___ ___ E ___ ___ ___
← ↓ ↓ ↗ ↓ →

WHICH WAY DO WE GO?
Answer Key

DIRECTION SECTION:

Beginning with the "n" in the lower left corner, follow the directional arrows to discover the next letter. Write the letters in the blanks provided to discover a hidden message.

F	O	A	T	O	I	U	Y
A	F	G	N	R	W	D	F
N	O	E	A	D	A	K	J
Y	N	E	V	T	E	K	A
X	C	V	A	N	B	T	N
C	E	R	B	C	T	O	X
W	V	B	T	E	Y	Q	Z
V	E	M	T	R	B	V	C
N	J	G	H	H	J	K	L

Answer Key: Never Try To Take Advantage of Anyone.

CIRCLE IT UP
CHARACTER EDUCATION PUZZLE

Grade Level: 3rd - Middle School

Time: 15 minutes per puzzle

Purpose: To teach children lessons on character education

Materials Needed: Copies of puzzles for everyone

Object: To complete the puzzle and discover the answer

Procedures:
- Hand out the puzzles to the class.
- Ask the students to complete the puzzles and discover the secret messages hidden within the puzzles.
- Share with the class the answers and discuss what the puzzle actually means.

FOLLOW-UP:

How can the strategies in the puzzle help build good character? Give examples.

CIRCLE IT UP

Note the number written under the blank and locate it beside the inter-connecting circles. Write the corresponding alphabet letter in the appropriate blank. When <u>one number</u> is written below a blank, find the <u>one number</u> written to the right of the circles and write the letter written in the corresponding circle on the blank. <u>If two numbers</u> of written below a blank, find the <u>two blank numbers</u> on the chart and write the letter that is written in the circle connecting the two letters.

Try to discover a great character building strategy.

___ ___   ___ ___ ___ ___   ___ ___   ___ ___ ___ ___ ___
9,10 9   8 ,9 8 7,8 7   6,7 6   5,6 9 6 5,6 5 9

___ ___ ___   ___ ___ ___   ___ ___ ___ ___ ___ ___ ___ ___ ___
4,5 4 6   3,4 3 9   2,3 8 2 2 9 3 9 7,8 6,7

___ ___ ___ ___   ___ ___ ___ Albert Einstein
2 3 6 1,2   1 6 10

CIRCLE IT UP
Answer Key

Note the number written under the blank and locate it beside the inter-connecting circles. Write the corresponding alphabet letter in the appropriate blank. When <u>one number</u> is written below a blank, find the <u>one number</u> written to the right of the circles and write the letter written in the corresponding circle on the blank. <u>If two numbers</u> of written below a blank, find the <u>two blank numbers</u> on the chart and write the letter that is written in the circle connecting the two letters.

Try to discover a great character building strategy

B	E		K	I	N	D		T	O		P	E	O	P	L	E
9,10	9		8 ,9	8	7,8	7		6,7	6		5,6	9	6	5,6	5	9

W	H	O		A	R	E		D	I	F	F	E	R	E	N	T
4,5	4	6		3,4	3	9		2,3	8	2	2	9	3	9	7,8	6,7

F	R	O	M		Y	O	U	
2	3	6	1,2		1	6	10	Albert Einstein

CIRCLE IT UP

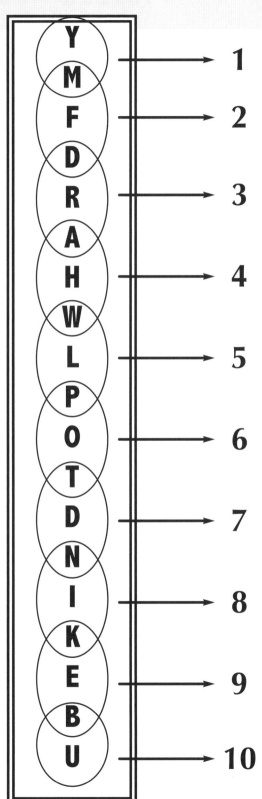

Y
M
F
D
R
A
H
W
L
P
O
T
D
N
I
K
E
B
U

1
2
3
4
5
6
7
8
9
10

Code Key:
1= y
1,2= m
2= f
2,3= d

ACTIONS SPEAK LOUDER THAN WORDS PUZZLE

Grade Level: 3rd - Middle School

Time: 15 minutes per puzzle

Purpose: To teach children lessons on character education

Materials Needed: Copies of puzzles for everyone

Object: To complete the puzzle and discover the answer

Procedures:

1. Hand out the puzzles to the class.

2. Ask the students to complete the puzzles and discover the secret messages hidden within the puzzles.

3. Share with the class the answers and discuss what the puzzle actually means.

FOLLOW-UP:

1. How would these words help you in life?
2. What would happen if you did these things everyday?
3. What are some other nice things you could do for other people?
4. Name someone in class who has done one of these things for you.

ACTIONS SPEAK LOUDER THAN WORDS

Try to find the words listed below in the puzzle. The words are located either vertically (up and down) or horizontally (left to right.) Circle the phrases as you find them.

All of the words are great things you can do to be a good friend. They are positive behaviors and help you be a better person. After you find them in the chart, look for them in your friends and in yourself. Remember that in the puzzle the phrases do not have spaces between the words.

D	S	C	C	C	M	B	B	E	B	E
F	D	S	H	A	R	E	E	R	E	D
B	C	A	C	R	J	T	A	E	H	E
N	D	Y	B	E	H	H	F	R	O	D
B	E	K	I	N	D	A	R	E	N	E
E	L	I	S	T	E	N	I	R	E	O
L	F	N	N	H	G	K	E	E	S	B
O	D	D	L	H	F	F	N	W	T	E
Y	W	W	P	H	D	U	S	D	G
A	E	O	L	G	F	L	G	E	C	E
L	R	R	K	H	D	T	G	E	C	N
K	E	D	J	B	E	N	I	C	E	T
L	W	S	H	G	F	G	V	D	D	L
L	O	V	E	O	T	H	E	R	S	E

Be kind	Be thankful	Be honest
Say kind words	Be a friend	Care
Listen	Give	Be loyal
Share	Be nice	Be gentle
	Love others	

ACTIONS SPEAK LOUDER THAN WORDS
Answer Key

Try to find the words listed below in the puzzle. The words are located either vertically (up and down) or horizontally (left to right.) Circle the phrases as you find them.

All of the words are great things you can do to be a good friend. They are positive behaviors and help you be a better person. After you find them in the chart, look for them in your friends and in yourself. Remember that in the puzzle the phrases do not have spaces between the words.

D	S	C	C	C	M	B	B	E	B	E
F	D	S	H	A	R	E	E	R	E	D
B	C	A	C	R	J	T	A	E	H	E
N	D	Y	B	E	H	H	F	R	O	D
B	E	K	I	N	D	A	R	E	N	E
E	L	I	S	T	E	N	I	R	E	O
L	F	N	N	H	G	K	E	E	S	B
O	D	D	L	H	F	F	N	W	T	E
Y	W	W	P	H	D	U	D	S	D	G
A	E	O	L	G	F	L	G	E	C	E
L	R	R	K	H	D	T	G	E	C	N
K	E	D	J	B	E	N	I	C	E	T
L	W	S	H	G	F	G	V	D	D	L
L	O	V	E	O	T	H	E	R	S	E

Be kind

Say kind words

Listen

Share

Be thankful

Be a friend

Give

Be nice

Love others

Be honest

Care

Be loyal

Be gentle

SKIPPING AROUND
CHARACTER EDUCATION PUZZLE

Grade Level: 3rd - Middle School

Time: 15 minutes per puzzle

Purpose: To teach children lessons on character education

Materials Needed: Copies of puzzles for everyone

Object: To complete the puzzle and discover the answer

Procedures:

1. Hand out the puzzles to the class.

2. Ask the students to complete the puzzles and discover the secret messages hidden within the puzzles.

3. Share with the class the answers and discuss what the puzzle actually means.

FOLLOW-UP:

1. What do you think this means with study skills?
2. What kinds of things do you think you should do?
3. What is the hardest thing to do when doing your homework?
4. What can you tell yourself to become more successful in school?
5. What can you do to help yourself get better in school?

Encourage students to write down good things that they can do to increase their study habits.

SKIPPING AROUND PUZZLE

Beginning with the T on the first box in the first column, follow the directions below to find a sentence about character education.

For example: Beginning with the K in the first box, follow the directions below to find a word about character.

K	B	I	M	N	I	D	O	P	P	P	P

First letter   K
Skip 1 space   I   Word: **KIND**
Skip 1 space   N
Skip 1 space   D

SKIPPING AROUND PUZZLE

T	T	R	K	Y	X	T	Y	O	H	D	O
T	H	H	J	I	C	N	T	G	G	S	V
Y	K	Q	O	K	V	U	R	B	F	X	C
T	L	H	N	I	B	N	E	K	D	C	X
Y	O	W	M	O	N	M	W	U	S	V	Z
C	M	A	N	N	M	N	Q	O	A	T	A

First Line: First word: Begin with T, Skip one space _____, Skip one space _____
Second word: Skip one space_____, Skip one space _____
Third word: Skip one space _____, Skip zero spaces_____

Second Line: Begin with T, Skip one space ____, Skip one space ____, Skip one space____ , Skip one space ____, Skip one space ___

Third Line: Begin with Y, Skip two spaces _____, Skip two spaces _____

Fourth Line: Begin with T, Skip one space ____, Skip one space ____, Skip one space ____ Skip one space ____

Fifth Line: Begin with Y, Skip three spaces _____, Skip three spaces _____

Sixth Line: Begin with C, Skip one space ____, Skip one space ____, Skip one space ____, Skip one space ____, Skip one space ____

Sentence: by Eleanor Roosevelt

_____ _____ _____ _____

_____ _____ _____ _____.

158

© YouthLight, Inc.

SKIPPING AROUND PUZZLE
Answer Key

T	T	R	K	Y	X	T	Y	O	H	D	O
T	H	H	J	I	C	N	T	G	G	S	V
Y	K	Q	O	K	V	U	R	B	F	X	C
T	L	H	N	I	B	N	E	K	D	C	X
Y	O	W	M	O	N	M	W	U	S	V	Z
C	M	A	N	N	M	N	Q	O	A	T	A

Answer to Puzzle:

First Line: Try to do
Second Line: things
Third Line: you
Fourth Line: think
Fifth line: you
Sixth line: cannot.

Try to do things you think you cannot. —*E. Roosevelt*

MOVING ON

Grade Level: 3rd - Middle School

Time: 30 minutes

Purpose: To help students differentiate between positive and negative situations.
To help students learn to stop and think in negative or dangerous situations

Object: To collect the most points by being the first to cross the finish line

Materials Needed: Question cards reproduced and cut out, twenty pieces of large construction paper to make the pattern on the floor for the game, die

Procedures:

1. Prepare the room for the activity by cutting ten pieces of construction paper in half. If possible, laminate the construction paper for durability. Then, place the paper on the floor in two straight rows of ten.

2. Mix positive and negative Game Cards and place them in a stack.

3. Divide students into two teams and ask each team to send a member up front. One member of each team will stand on the first square of their rows.

4. Begin by choosing a student from each team to take turns, and read a card from the Game Cards stack. If the student reads a card that represents a negative situation or character trait, ask the person standing on the paper row to STOP or remain in place. If the student reads a card that represents a positive trait or social skill, allow the student a chance to GO or move forward. To determine the number of spaces the student can move, ask the student holding the card to roll a die and then ask the student standing to move forward the number of spaces indicated on the die. Discuss why each situation is positive or negative and what a student might think or do in the situation. Then the other team follows the same procedure.

5. Award the team that first crosses the end of the row ten points. If the other team has not had an even number of turns, allow them a final roll. If they also cross the finish line at this time, award this team ten points as well. If they do not cross the finish line after completing the roll, do not award any points to the team.

6. Begin another round by having two new team members begin on square one of each team's row. Two new team members can also be the new card readers. Continue playing as time allows.

FOLLOW-UP:

Ask students the following questions:
1. What situation is most difficult to stop and think about?
2. What situation is easiest to stop and think about?
3. When is it hard to walk away?
4. When is it hard to do something positive when everyone else is doing something negative?
5. What is the secret of maintaining self-control?
6. What happens when you do something that you know is wrong?
7. What happens when you do something that you know is right?

MOVING ON GAME CARDS

Someone rolls his/her eyes at you. You tell them to stop or you'll punch them.

You help someone who is new to your school by introducing her to your friends.

You are honest.

You turn in your homework every day.

You walk away from someone who makes a bad comment to you.

You ask a person to leave you alone in a firm way.

You hit someone because you don't like him.

You make fun of someone because she can't throw a ball.

You make a joke about someone from a different country.

© YouthLight, Inc.

MOVING ON GAME CARDS

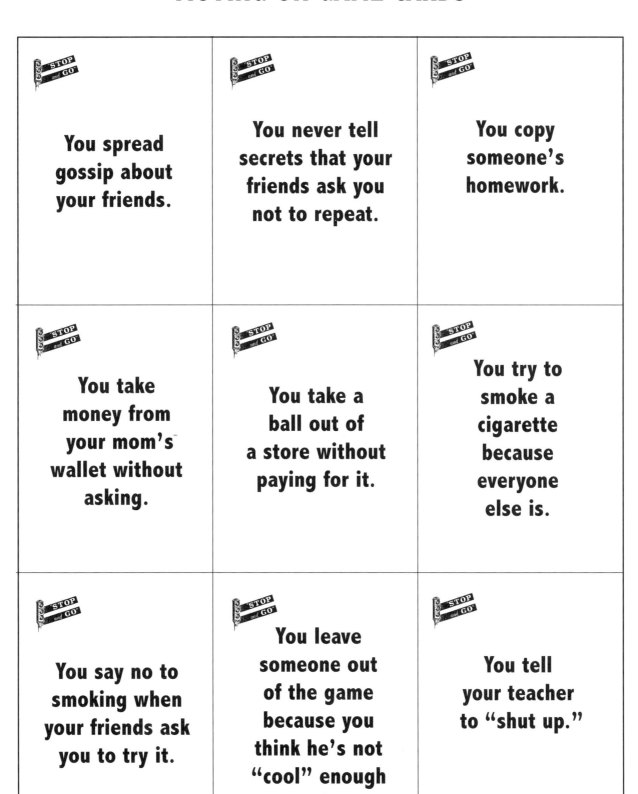

You spread gossip about your friends.

You never tell secrets that your friends ask you not to repeat.

You copy someone's homework.

You take money from your mom's wallet without asking.

You take a ball out of a store without paying for it.

You try to smoke a cigarette because everyone else is.

You say no to smoking when your friends ask you to try it.

You leave someone out of the game because you think he's not "cool" enough to play.

You tell your teacher to "shut up."

MOVING ON GAME CARDS

STOP and GO You are polite to your teacher.	**STOP and GO** You are respectful to adults.	**STOP and GO** You help your grandmother with her yard.
STOP and GO You say please and thank you.	**STOP and GO** You push people out of the way.	**STOP and GO** You make fun of others who don't speak the same language you do.
STOP and GO You try to take time to get to know others who are different from you.	**STOP and GO** You share your things with others.	**STOP and GO** You give some of your old things to Good Will to help others.

MOVING ON GAME CARDS

STOP and GO **You are polite in the cafeteria.**	STOP and GO **You like to get in fights.**	STOP and GO **You like to act like you don't care about school.**
STOP and GO **You never do your homework.**	STOP and GO **You always bring everything you need for class.**	STOP and GO **You like to pull other people's hair to aggravate them.**
STOP and GO **You threaten others.**	STOP and GO **You bully other students.**	STOP and GO **You invite someone to eat with you who doesn't seem to have a friend.**

MOVING ON GAME CARDS

 You play with someone on the playground that doesn't have anyone to play with.

 You are truthful.

 You call someone stupid.

 You give someone a compliment.

 You listen when others speak.

 You talk about how people look in a mean way.

ALL TANGLED UP

Grade Level: 3rd - Middle School

Time: 30 minutes

Purpose: To demonstrate that our lives are all interconnected and we become stronger friends when we do kind things for each other

Object: To toss the yarn around the circle while telling about positive character traits

Materials Needed: ball of yarn - (roll yarn around in a small circle until it becomes a little ball)

Procedures:

1. Ask the students to sit in a circle.

2. Toss the ball of yarn around from student to student to eventually form a "web." Before a student can throw the ball or yarn, ask the student to answer one of the questions listed below. The leader may randomly ask the questions before each person throws the ball or just choose two or three questions to concentrate on during the activity.
   - State something positive that can be done to help the class, the community, or their family.
   - Tell about a famous person who has done something to help the world.
   - Tell about someone that you know who has done something to help the community or their family.
   - Tell about something that you have done to help someone in some way.
   - Tell something positive about the person to whom you are throwing the ball.
   - Tell about a positive character trait (like hard work, honesty, etc.).
   - Tell why you think positive behaviors are important.
   - Tell about a career that depends on positive character traits.

FOLLOW-UP:

After every person has participated in the activity and is holding a piece of the yarn, ask the following questions:

- Do you think this one ball of yarn connects us all?
- Since we didn't all throw the ball to each other, why might you think that we are connected?
- In real life, are all the students in this room connected in some way? How?
- Do you think connections are formed when we do good things and when we do bad things? How?
- How do you feel when someone connects with you by doing something nice for you?
- How do you feel when someone connects with you by doing something a little mean to you?
- Do you think the world is made a better place by the nicer connections or by the meaner connections?

- What do you think we could all do to make sure our classroom is a nicer place for connections?
- (Ask one student to drop their piece of yarn. Emphasize what happens to the web when this happens - not as pretty, looser, a little messed up.) What happens when one person in our class does something not so nice? How does that affect our class?
- How does bullying and teasing affect the connections or friendships in our class?
- How does gossiping affect the connections or friendships in our class?
- What kind of agreement might we come up with in order to make our class a better place for making friends?

LIGHTS, CAMERA, ACTION

Grade Level: 3rd - Middle School

Time: 30 minutes

Purpose: To demonstrate positive character traits by acting out a story

Object: To take the objects in a bag and develop a skit to demonstrate a positive character attribute. To be the group that gets the most points by using all the items in the bag to make up the story.

Materials Needed: small bags with various items placed in them (wallets, sunglasses, play money, watches, etc.) Place equal numbers of items in each bag. Make enough bags for the number of groups you will have.

Procedures:

1. Divide the class into small groups of 4 or 5.

2. Give each group a small bag with various items placed in each bag. Vary the number of items depending on the age of the children.

3. Challenge each group to create a skit using the items in the bag to demonstrate a positive character trait or good decision making skills. Award the group 50 points for each item they use in their skit. Challenge each group to see which group can get the most points. For example, consider a scenario in which the following items are placed in the bag: wallet, key, food item, book, phone.

   The skit might go something like this:
   A boy is on his way home from school carrying his book when he comes upon a wallet lying on the sidewalk. He looks around and doesn't see anyone for one block going each way, so he picks up the wallet and looks inside. When he looks inside, he notices a key, which looks very small and different from other keys. The boy wonders what the key can be and rushes home. He picks up the phone and calls his best friend to ask him what to do. "Look for a number in the wallet and let your parents call the wallet's owner. It may be a very important key," his friend says. So the boy decides to wait on his parents to come home. He gets himself a little snack (food item) to eat while he waits. Eventually his mom and dad come home and call the number. A lady answers the phone. She is so excited that someone has found her wallet and key. She tells the boy that the key opened her grandmother's trunk, which had many beautiful family pictures and special things inside. Thanks to the boy's good decision making skills, she can now get into the trunk without tearing up the trunk.

   The possibilities for skits are endless.

4. Ask the students to act out the skit and then to discuss the morals or positive character traits they presented in the story.

FOLLOW-UP:

1. Ask the students to individually write the story. This will further emphasize writing skills that many teachers are working on in these particular grade levels.
2. Ask the students to write a paper about the morals presented in each story.
3. Ask students the following questions about the stories:
   - Where in the stories could the main character have made a different choice?
   - How would this have mattered?
   - Do you sometimes have choices like this to make in your life?
   - How do you know what is the right thing to do?
   - Who do you know that sets a good example for making right choices?

WHAT WOULD THEY DO?

Grade Level: 3rd - Middle School

Time: Two sessions - One session to explain and work on project
One session to share results of project

Purpose:
• To encourage students to see difficult situations from other people's perspectives
• To encourage students to think of great people in life and how they have overcome difficult situations
• To develop positive character traits like responsibility, honesty, and respect when confronting difficult situations

Materials Needed: Index card

Object: To do reports on famous people in order to determine the famous person's good character trait and to answer the situation cards as to how that famous person would react

Procedures:

1. Explain the concept of having good character traits. Ask students to brainstorm a list of famous people in history they admire for having good character. Explain the concept of good character.

2. Assign each student a famous person, and ask him or her to write a brief paragraph answering the following questions. You may want to assign this as a homework assignment or as a class assignment. Ask the students to answer the following questions about their assigned person.
   a. For what was the person famous?
   b. What positive character traits did this person possess? (honesty, cooperation, leadership, etc.)
   After initial research, ask students to write one paragraph about when this person demonstrated these character traits to help other people. Ask students to write the on a large index card. Be sure to write the name of the famous person on the card.

3. Collect the reports and place the cards in a basket.

4. Take turns calling up student volunteers. Ask the volunteer to complete the following directions:
   a. Choose a card from the basket.
   b. Read the report to the class.
   c. Ask the volunteer to answer one of the following questions based on what he/she believes that famous person would do?
      • What would this person do if someone wanted him/her to fight?
      • What would this person do if someone were making fun of someone who was different?
      • What would this person do if someone tried to get them to drink alcohol?
      • What would this person do if someone called his or her mother a name?
      • What would this person do if someone tried to gossip to them?
      • What would this person do if someone talked about his or her best friend?

- What would this person do if he/she were given homework assignments?
- What would this person do if his/her parents asked him/her to do chores?
- What would this person do if he/she accidentally broke out a window?
- What would this person do if he/she were faced with the choice of smoking a cigarette?

5. Continue reading cards until all cards have been discussed.

FOLLOW-UP:

1. Do you think it's important to have role models in our lives? Why or why not?
2. Can you think of people on TV who do good things now? Name some examples.
3. Can you think of people on TV who do not set a good example? Name some examples.
4. Is it important to study people who do good things? Why?
5. Is it important to study people who do not do good things? Why?
6. Is it more important to hang around people who do things the right way or the wrong way?
7. Could your friend's actions have an effect on your actions?
8. Have you ever been in trouble because you were with the wrong people at the wrong time?

Study Skills

Study Skills

More and more legislation on both state and federal levels has placed emphasis on the achievement levels of students in all grades. Specifically, the "No Child Left Behind" legislation has placed a high priority on students being on grade level and achieving certain basic levels of knowledge. In order to achieve these goals set by state and federal governments, students in our schools must develop the ability to recall information and recognize the information on state, national, and local tests. While the goals maintain high expectations for all students to learn, it is necessary to develop practical skills to enable students to meet these standards.

Study skills are necessary for children to be successful not only in reaching local and federal baseline goals, but also in developing skills necessary for a competitive work force. The strategies presented in this chapter will help students to accomplish these goals by presenting easy "tricks" to help students remember words, phrases, and lists. The activities also encourage the development of positive skills in the classroom and at home in order to provide students with the necessary tools for success. These tools will provide crucial skills that will help students increase their ability to take tests, and achieve higher scores, and decrease the anxiety for not performing well on important tests given in the classroom.

ELECTRIC SLIDE

Grade Level: 3rd - Middle School

Time: 30 minutes

Materials Needed: None

Purpose: To practice a Mnemonic memory technique

Object: To create a sentence

Procedures:

1. Ask the class members to share the ways that help them to remember things that they need to learn. Review the visual learning technique in the Lickity Split Lesson if that has been covered.

2. Present the sentence technique of learning things in order. For example, to learn the names of the nine planets, you may use a sentence such as, My Very Eager Mother Just Served Us Nine Pizzas. Tell students that the first letter of each word in the sentence is the first letter of each of the nine planets, Mercury, Venus, Earth, Mars, Jupiter, Saturn, Uranus, Neptune, and Pluto. The same thing can be done for difficult spelling words, such as geography. The sentence could be, George eats old, green rats at Phil's house yard. Remind the students that the sentence must be one that can be pictured.

3. Divide into small groups of three. Give each group a difficult word to learn to spell or a list of something to learn in order such as a grocery list, bird names, pet names, etc.

4. Let the small groups create a sentence to go with the first letter of each letter in the spelling word or the first letter of each word in a list.

5. Allow each group to share the sentence that they created in order to learn their spelling word or the list.

FOLLOW-UP:

Ask the class members to share how well the sentence picture clue helped in learning. What would help them more in learning something?

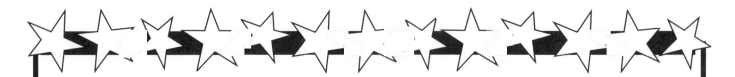

GIANT STEPS

Grade Level: 3rd - Middle School

Time: 30 minutes

Materials Needed: paper, pencils

Purpose: To recognize steps to take to reach a goal

Object: To write steps needed for a goal

Procedures:

1. Review Goal Setting and preparing for obstacles in reaching that goal.

2. Discuss the steps that are needed to reach a goal. For example, getting the materials together that will be needed, scheduling time to complete the goal, keeping a positive attitude toward the goal, etc. Are all steps necessary to reach a goal?

3. Divide the class into small groups of four or five. Make sure that each team is allowed to have the same number of turns. Therefore, be aware that some team members will need to go more than one time.

4. Distribute paper to the first person on each team. The team needs to go in the same order each time.

5. Call out a practice situation with a sample educational goal such as bringing up math grades. Ask the students to share the steps in order and number the steps on the board as to what needs to be done before reaching that goal. Emphasize the following suggestions:
   • Keep all materials needed together (paper, pencil, math book, etc.)
   • Know the directions and understand them.
   • Ask for help from a teacher, friend or a parent when the material is not understood.
   • Work in a quiet place without interruptions.
   • Set a timer or have a watch to set a time limit to finish the goal.
   • Complete all homework, and turn it in on time.

6. Call out a new educational goal. Ask each person in each group to take turns writing and numbering a step that needs to be taken toward that goal. Ask group members to circulate the sheet clockwise in the group until everyone has had a turn. Remind group members that occasionally someone may need to correct a step that is listed that may be out of place. There is no group discussion for this activity. Allow 3 minutes before time is up.

7. Ask the first group who finished to share the steps on the paper. Encourage the other groups to share any changes or corrections to the list.

8. Continue with another goal and ask the groups to continue writing the steps as before and sharing together as they have done previously.

FOLLOW-UP:

Discuss how breaking down steps toward a goal can help a person reach that goal. Are steps necessary in reaching a goal?

HAPPY DAYS

Grade Level: 2nd - Middle School

Time: 30 minutes

Materials Needed: Spelling list, paper, pencils, make 3 x 5 Smiley Face Cards

Purpose: To learn to study by self-checking

Object: To spell correctly

Procedures:

1. Review ways to remember things that need to be learned such as the visual rhyming technique and the sentence picture clue technique which are in the lessons Lickity Split and Electric Slide.

2. Present the self-checking technique of learning things. Give each person a sheet of notebook paper, and ask student to fold the paper in half long ways. Write a difficult spelling word on the board. Ask each person to copy the correct spelling of the word on the left inside of the folded paper and to study spelling the word by themselves for a few seconds. Remind the class not to write darkly.

3. Ask each person to close the folded paper in order to write on the back left side of the folded paper. The paper must always be folded.

4. Erase the word from the board and call out the same word. Ask each class member to write it down from memory.

5. Ask each person to self-check him/herself by referring back to the first copies of the correct spelling on the inside left. Challenge them to determine if what they wrote from memory matches the correct spelling. If it does not, ask them go to the back left side again to try again to write the word correctly.

6. Divide into small groups of four or five.

7. Call out another difficult spelling word and write the correct spelling on the board for the groups to copy on the folded paper under the practice word. Ask each person to study the word by him/herself. Then erase the word from the board, and call out the word again. Ask each group to turn to the back left side as with the practice word, and write the same word from memory. Ask them to look back at the inside left to check the correctness of the second spelling.

8. Appoint a checker from each group to go around to each member of the checker's group to check accuracy. The group members may take turns being a checker.

9. Ask each group to come up to get a happy face card for each correct spelling in that group.

FOLLOW-UP:

Discuss other ways in which self-checking can help with learning.

JITTER BUG

Grade Level: 3rd - Middle School

Time: 30 minutes

Materials Needed: Notebook paper, notebook (3 ring), pencils, ruler, class books dividers, etc. (These can be donated for the lesson by the students.)

Purpose: To practice organizing study materials

Object: To organize study materials quickly & also to be able to recognize when study materials are disorganized

Procedures:

1. Discuss organizing study materials. What materials are needed? Where should the materials be located?

2. Select two teams, certain tables or rows versus the other set of tables or rows.

3. Place study materials such as notebook paper, dividers, notebook, pencils, ruler, class books (everything needed as materials for studying) on a table.

4. Call three people up to the front of the room from each team.

5. Decide which team places everything in disarray (Mess Up Team) and which team will straighten up the study materials. (Organizing Team)

6. Give the Mess Up Team 15 seconds to put everything out of order. Give the Organizing Team 30 seconds to organize the study material.

7. Award a winning point to the Organizing Team for that round if the Mess Up Team finds nothing out of place.

8. Begin the next round by calling up three more people from each team and changing duties.

FOLLOW-UP:

Discuss which was easier, to mess the study materials up or to organize them. Why is it important to have study materials in place and organized?

LICKITY SPLIT

Grade Level: 2nd - Middle School

Time: 30 minutes

Materials Needed: Category Lists

Purpose: To practice visual learning in order to remember lists

Object: To stay at the front of a line by reporting lists correctly

Procedures:

1. Ask the class to discuss the best way that they know to memorize something such as lists, spelling words, etc.

2. Present the visual learning technique of word pictures. This requires matching something you want to remember with a rhyming word and a picture in your head. You could even draw the picture. For example, one - bun; two - shoe; three - tree; four - door; five - hive; six - sticks; seven - oven; eight - gate; nine - line; ten - hen. Have the group practice these ten items with a partner in close proximity for 30 seconds.

3. Call on a few volunteers who would like to repeat the ten rhyming picture clues aloud.

4. Divide into small groups of four or six members. Let the groups again practice with a partner in that group the same ten rhyming picture clues.

5. Have a group line up in front of the room. Start with the first person on the left as the group faces the class in order to go from left to right. The first person must say the list of ten items. The first person may keep that position if the list is repeated correctly. If the list is not repeated correctly, ask the first person to go to the end of the group line, giving the second person a chance to say the list correctly and stay in first position. Challenge each group member to try to stay near the front of the line. If more than one person in a row repeats the list correctly, ask the members to continue to remain near the front of the line and to remember the order of the members.

6. Give new words to add to the list of ten to continually keep it challenging. Be sure the groups get practice time for the new lists. For example, a grocery list such as, one-bun-green beans can be visualized. Picture the green beans inside of the bun. Two-shoe-oranges; picture the oranges inside of a shoe. Other types of lists include types of sports, names of planets, names of teams, etc.

7. Continue calling up each group to repeat the new list, and to determine the ones near the front of the line.

8. Change the list to a new category to add a new challenge.

FOLLOW-UP:

How can this visual learning technique help someone learn? What helped you to learn the lists? Was it practice, visualizing, or writing it down in words or in pictures?

CATEGORY LISTS

SPORTS: football, soccer, basketball, baseball, tennis, gymnastics, golf, swimming, horseback riding, car racing

GROCERY LIST: peas, green beans, squash, hamburger, lettuce, bread, butter, jelly, catsup, milk

BIRDS: canary, black bird, cardinal, wren, blue bird, black bird, parrot, sea gull, dove, mocking bird

DOGS: Spaniel, Shepherd, Poodle, Greyhound, Dachshund, Scottie, Sheltie, Pit Bull, Collie, Lab

FLOWERS: rose, daffodil, violet, pansy, carnation, daisy, mum, azalea, lily, iris

GAMES: Monopoly™, Uno™, Candyland™, Chutes & Ladders™, Rummy, Go Fish™, Old Maid™, Checkers™, Trivia

TOYS: Lego's™, doll, toy gun, match cars, dollhouse, tea set, ball, skates, bike, scooter

PETS: dog, cat, parakeet, hamster, iguana, turtle, pot-bellied pig, mouse, gold fish, ferret

TOOLS: hammer, screw driver, pliers, wrench, nail, screw, drill, saw, ruler, level

SUBJECTS: math, spelling, writing, language, art, reading, social studies, science, music, computers

LINE DANCE

Grade Level: 3rd - Middle School

Time: 30 minutes

Materials Needed: Direction Cards

Purpose: To learn to follow directions

Object: To perform a line dance with a group

Procedures:

1. Discuss things you need to do when you are following directions. Emphasize good listening, good attitude, accepting authority, reading and rereading written directions, asking questions to clarify, checking directions as you work, writing down oral directions, etc.

2. Divide the class into small groups of three to four.

3. Give each group a direction card that contains Line Dance steps.

4. Provide time for the groups to read the directions and discuss or ask questions. (Approximately three minutes.)

5. Tell the groups to begin practicing the directions. In order to be able to perform the directions for the class. Allow five minutes.

6. Move around to each group to check participation and accuracy of understanding.

7. Give each group a chance to perform their Line Dance directions. (Music is optional.)

FOLLOW-UP:

Discuss what happened in each group as they began to follow the directions. What parts were good, and what parts didn't work?

LINE DANCE CARDS

LINE DANCE CARD 1

Two steps left, two steps right
Lean forward, lean back,
Walk three steps forward, walk three steps backward,
Turn two times to the left & clap once,
Turn two times to the right & clap once
Bow!

LINE DANCE CARD 2

Turn around to the left one time,
Turn around to the right one time,
Hop three times forward,
Hop three times backward,
Slide three times to the left,
Slide three times to the right,
Hop four times and kneel down.
Stand up and bow.

LINE DANCE CARD 3

Clap four times over your head,
Clap four times at your waist,
Clap four times at your ankles,
Turn around three times to the left,
Turn around three times to the right,
Slide two times to the front,
Slide two times to the back,
Wiggle once and jump up & bow!

LINE DANCE CARDS

LINE DANCE CARD 4

Turn to your right and bow,
Turn to your left and bow, Face forward and bow,
Raise your hands over your head and wave,
Lower your hands to the floor and pat,
March in place six times,
Turn to face the back and march in place six times,
Jump high three times,
Bow!

LINE DANCE CARD 5

Put your left foot out and bring it back,
Put your right foot out and bring it back,
Wave your hands over your head and turn around,
Clap four times,
Put your head down, put your head up,
Slide two times to the right,
Slide two times to the left,
Wave your hands over your head and turn around,
Bow!

LINE DANCE CARD 6

Skip forward two times,
Turn & skip back in place two times,
Shake your right side,
Shake your left side,
Walk around in a small circle at your place,
Tap your right toe three times,
Tap your left toe three times,
Bow!

OBSTACLE COURSE

Grade Level: 3rd - Middle School

Time: 30 minutes

Materials Needed: Obstacle Course Sheet per student

Purpose: To know the problems that keep a person from reaching a goal

Object: To fill in an Obstacle Course Sheet

Procedures:

1. Review and give examples of setting educational goals.

2. Discuss the problems that come up to keep a person from reaching a goal. For example, a goal of making a higher math grade may not be reached due to too much time spent watching TV.

3. Pass out a Race Sheet for each student. Explain each flag on the Race Sheet. A yellow flag (triangle) tells a person to be careful of something. A green flag (square) tells you to Go, but also tells you that you need to determine where you are going. A red flag (double triangle) means you are in Danger of not reaching a goal. A black and white flag (checkered) is at the Finish Line to show the goal has been accomplished.

4. Write what you would like to set as an educational goal in the box by the green flag. Ask for students to share some examples and encourage them to be specific.

5. Give 1 minute for Goal Setting. Let each student turn to a student close by to share the goal with each other. Ask the students to share the partner's goal aloud to the class.

6. Give one minute for the yellow flag. Ask students to write in the box by the yellow flag something that might be a problem or hindrance in reaching their goal. Give an example or a hindrance such as not controlling the urge to talk to friends during the lesson. After completing this task, ask each student to turn to the same student as before and share what was written in the box. Ask the students to share the partner's Caution aloud to the class, and give a suggestion as to what to do about the Caution situation.

7. Give one minute to write down the biggest Danger that would hinder that person from reaching the Goal. Write the answer in the box by the red flag. Turn to the previous partner to share this danger. Ask the students to share the partner's Danger aloud to the class, and give a suggestion on how to deal with that danger.

8. Give one minute to write down in the box by the black and white flag. What would happen if you got to the Finish Line and completed your Goal? How would your life be different? Share the answer with the previous partner, and then share aloud with the class how your life would be different by achieving the Goal.

FOLLOW-UP:

Why is it important to recognize problems before you get to them? Why do racecar drivers look for possible problems on a racecourse before they even begin the race?

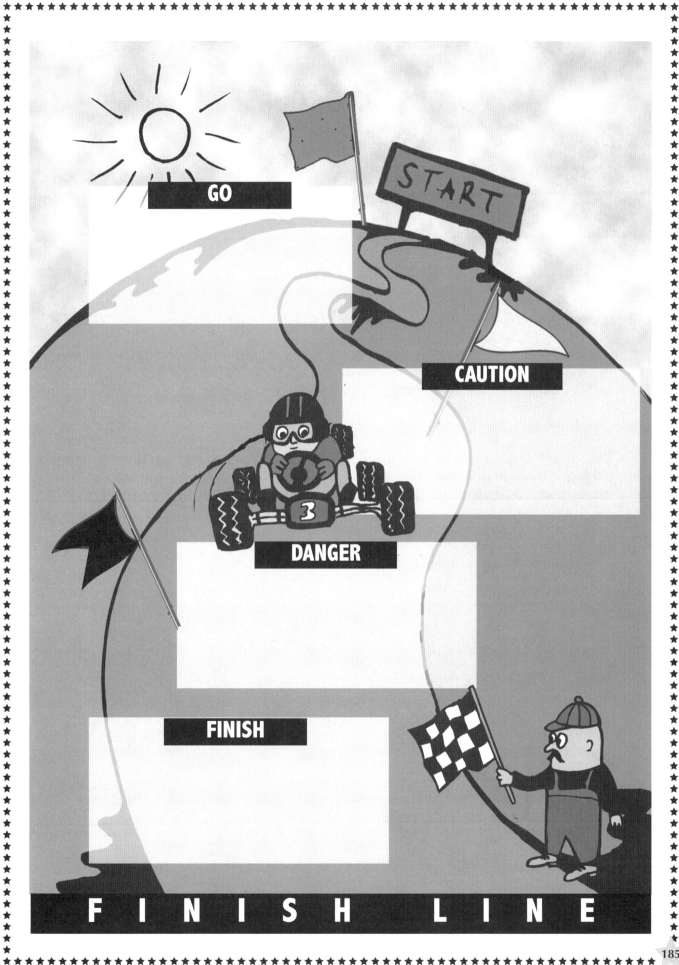

GO

START

CAUTION

DANGER

3

FINISH

F I N I S H   L I N E

RAP TIME

Grade Level: 3rd - Middle School

Time: 30 minutes

Materials Needed: pencils, paper

Purpose: To review study skills

Object: To create a rap on Study Skills

Procedures:

1. Review the skills needed for good study skills or habits. Bring out characteristics such as having a good attitude, organizing study materials, practicing good listening, following directions, setting educational goals, managing time, following a schedule, etc.

2. Divide the students into small groups of three or four members.

3. Encourage them to create a rap, which does or does not rhyme, about one of the main study skills that is needed for good study results. Do a short one together as a whole class. Write it on the board as the students share their ideas.

4. Begin the group work on their raps about study skills. Allow 4 - 5 minutes.

5. Provide time for each group to come up front to present the rap.

FOLLOW-UP:

Ask the class what they learned about study skills and the importance of developing and working on these skills.

ROCK AROUND THE CLOCK

Grade Level: 2nd - Middle School

Time: 30 Minutes

Materials Needed: Clock Sheets, paper gray rocks or real pebbles Study Schedule Item List

Purpose: To learn how to organize study time

Object: To put a rock by each clock

Procedures:

1. Discuss making a study schedule. Emphasize that a study schedule helps a student get the studying, homework, and projects finished on time and turned into the teacher for the best possible grade.

2. Ask students to write their name on the clock sheet that is given to them.

3. Call out a Schedule Item from the list. Have the students write this item on top of the first clock.

4. Ask each student to draw the hands on the first clock to show when he/she starts that Study Schedule Item.

5. Encourage some students to share the time that they begin a specific Study Schedule Item. (Example: Homework begins at 3:00.) Also, ask them to share why they do that Schedule Item at the particular time. The answers will be different due to different needs of the students. For example, some students don't get home from school until later or some may have sports activities to attend. Therefore, there is no right or wrong answer. Encourage the students to recognize good choices.

6. Ask one person in each row or table group to give their group or row a "rock" to place on the first clock if their time works for them.

7. Ask which students drew a time that doesn't work. Challenge them to go back and change it to a time that will work for them. These students may then have their group leader get a rock for them.

8. Move on to the second clock and repeat the same procedure with another schedule item. Repeat until all the clocks have been completed.

FOLLOW-UP:

Have a discussion with the group as to how necessary a Study Schedule would be in their day to day activities in school. Encourage the students to put this clock schedule in their notebooks for further reference.

SCHEDULE ITEM LIST

Snack time

Begin homework

End homework

Play

Eat supper

Watch TV

Read

**Pack your book bag
or get books together**

Get clothes ready for the next day

Talk on the phone

Go to bed

Get up the next day

CLOCK SHEET

TIME WARP

Grade Level: 2nd - Middle School

Time: 30 minutes

Materials Needed: paper, large yellow circle

Purpose: To set goals with a realistic, positive attitude

Objective: To fly a paper airplane close to the moon

Procedures:

1. Define the differences between a positive attitude and a realistic attitude. Emphasize that a person should try to determine his/her capabilities, strengths and weaknesses from family members, teachers, grades, and other sources.

2. Permit the class members to share some positive, realistic educational goals they might already have or would like to have.

3. Give each person a sheet of notebook paper or plain copy paper. Ask them to fold the paper into a plane that they can design themselves. Allow 3 minutes.

4. Tell each person to write one educational goal that they would like to accomplish on the plane.

5. Place the large, yellow circle on the floor at the front of the room. Tell the class that it represents the moon or reaching a goal that has been set.

6. Choose three students at a time to come to the front of the room. Ask each of these students to share the goal on his/her plane and the destination or place he/she wants to go.

7. Allow each of the three students to take turns flying his/her plane the closest to the moon to symbolize reaching their goal or destination.

8. Determine the winner by choosing the plane that lands the closest to the moon. Ask this person to stay up front while the other two students sit down. Ask two more students to come up to the front of the room and challenge the last champion. After winning three times in a row, that champion will retire. Begin again by calling up three new players.

FOLLOW-UP:

Ask the class how important it is for them to reach their goal. Did it make any difference in the plane's design as to whether each plane reached the moon goal? What are some things that make a difference in whether people reach a goal?

TWIST AGAIN

Grade Level: 3rd - Middle School

Time: 30 minutes

Materials Needed: Music (Optional)

Purpose: To practice good listening

Object: To stop when the signal indicates

Procedures:

1. Discuss what is involved in good listening, such as looking at the speaker or leader, having nothing around to distract, thinking about the topic at hand, sitting still, etc.

2. Explain that a beginning signal such as one clap or turning on music indicates when to begin twisting back and forth. A second signal such as three claps or turning the music off indicates when to stop twisting and freeze.

3. Select five people to come to the front of the room to Twist Again. Remind them to begin with the pre-decided signal and remind them to stop with a pre-decided signal.

4. Begin by reading aloud a situation that needs good listening, such as the teacher calling out the spelling word test. Then, give the signal for the group to twist for a few seconds before giving the signal to stop.

5. Find out what helped them to stop on signal. Ask why it's important to stop to listen in the situation read aloud.

6. Bring up a new group, and continue in the same manner.

FOLLOW-UP:

Discuss what can happen if the twisting or poor listening continues after the listening situation begins.

BOOT, SCOOT, & BOOGIE

Grade Level: 3rd - Middle School

Time: 30 minutes

Materials Needed: Boot sheets

Purpose: To make educational goals

Object: To fill up the Boot Sheet

Procedures:

1. Distribute the Boot Sheets to each person.

2. Read aloud the categories or steps on the boot.

3. Instruct each student to write an educational goal at the top of the boot that can be worked on during this grading period. Take time for the students to share the goals either with a neighbor or with the class.

4. Discuss each category or steps in educational goal setting. Discuss what is required in setting goals. Have the students give examples of each of the goal setting steps. The steps on the boot are:
   (1) Type of people who can help a person to reach a goal
   (2) Grades needed to reach the goal
   (3) Problems in reaching the goal
   (4) Sequential steps to take in order to reach the goal

5. Discuss the first step. Review its meaning. Ask each person to fill in the box beside that Step according to personal choice. Briefly discuss and share the different written responses that some of the students have in the step 1 box. A student may go back later to fill in any boxes left as the class moves on to the next step.

6. Read aloud step 2. Review its meaning. Continue in the same manner as with step 1. Continue until all of the steps have been filled in.

FOLLOW-UP:

This will be an ongoing sharing and discussion.

BOOT, SCOOT, & BOOGIE SHEET

Type of people who can help a person to reach a goal

_____
_____
_____
_____
_____

Grades needed to reach the goal

_____
_____
_____

Problems in reaching the goal

_____
_____
_____
_____
_____
_____
_____

Sequential steps to take in order to reach the goal

_____
_____
_____
_____
_____

★★

About the Authors

Kathy Cooper, MSW is currently a high school counselor and has worked as an elementary school counselor and social worker. In over twenty years of experience, she has been an innovator in the development of creative activities, strategies, and games that enable students to more effectively deal with problem situations in their lives. Kathy has presented seminars in more that 25 states and is the co-author of *Leave No Angry Child Behind, Power Play, Quality Time for Quality Kids, Innovative Strategies for Unlocking Difficult Children, Innovative Strategies for Unlocking Difficult Adolescents, Ready Freddie.* Kathy is also a National Board certified Counselor.

Marianne Vandawalker, M.Ed. is a recently retired school counselor with over thirty years of experience as a school counselor and teacher where she has developed many creative techniques for dealing with problems in the classroom. She also has a MED and certification in reading and language arts as well as counseling. Marianne has worked in crisis intervention and in family therapy and is the author of several books including *Character Fun, Career Fun, Power Play, What Do You Want To Be, Jungle Bullies, Study Skills Fun, ABC Careers, & Payday.*

Marianne reaches students with high interest material and activities. It is her goal to reach the counseling needs of various ages of young people through active classroom guidance and small group counseling. Both settings raise awareness and skills. Her lessons are used each day to try out the effect on students and teachers alike. Changes and improvements in students come through experiencing the lessons.